VOLUME I

The Cultural Context of Classroom Practice in American Schools

A Guide for All Teachers

by

Maxine Newsome, Ph.D.

*MODEL ALTERNATIVE SCHOOL SERVICES PROFESSIONAL DEVELOPMENT
SERIES FOR EXCELLENCE IN TEACHING AND LEARNING*

This series is dedicated to my late husband and friend, Thomas Newsome I, who was the wind beneath my wings in living through the topics and events of this series.

Copyright © 2012 by Maxine Newsome.
All rights reserved, including the right of reproduction in whole or in part or in any form.
ISBN   978-0-9839496-0-2
Published by MASS

Please visit www.schoolin.org for further consultation and inquiry.

MASS
Professional Development Series for Excellence in Teaching and Learning

CONTENTS

Volume I

The Context of Classroom Practice in American Schools

Volume II

Improving Classroom Practice Through Culturally-Inclusive Classroom Management

Volume III

Improving Classroom Practice Through a Culturally-Centered Education Program

Volume IV

Improving Classroom Practice Through Culturally-Transformative Teaching

"As the editor of this book and as a licensed educator in the public school system, I have deepened my understanding of what my population of students will require for growing through their transitions in my classrooms with joy and a sense of recognition—and of how I can be the greater teacher that I have not yet had the courage to be.

We all have to learn to come from the places that others come from and to be guests in those places, and to teach to those places in ourselves while holding them open for the interactions of others. With the authority of a caring friend on the journey to genuine and masterful teaching, the work will bring your thinking as an educator in today's world to another, more encompassing platform—so that we can all enjoy these new places of beauty together."

Erjan Slavin, Teacher, Author, Poet, Editor
--Peekskill, NY

"Building cross-cultural understanding for a caring world through excellence in classroom practice..."

Overview of the MASS Professional Development Series

"We can change the world!" is clearly a belief of many young people and is a major reason why many decide to enter the field of education. At no point in time has the challenge set forth in this rallying cry been more relevant than today as we look toward a Twenty-First Century world.

Now, the work begins. It involves the way that you, the teachers of America, take on this challenge through the practices that you employ in your classrooms. It has to do with your insight and ability to help students from multiple cultural backgrounds to learn, interact with each other, understand each other, and to care for and about each other.

Changing the world may seem like a lofty goal...but when you think about it, given the number of students with whom you will interact over the course of your career, you are positioned to change the lives of many. You will have students as your captive audience for more hours than any other of society's institutions, including the family. The way that you use your influence with your students in the classroom can make a lasting difference in what and how well they will learn, in their perceptions and attitudes, and in the way they will go out into the world and relate to others in the larger society. In this sense, as a classroom teacher, you can create a culturally-inclusive classroom to serve as a microcosm for building respect, understanding, and caring in a multicultural world. The power to change the society resides with you, a dedicated teacher, who nurtures your students to be the influential leaders of tomorrow. The lofty goal of changing the world will come only when you have the vision of what it can be, and acknowledge the powerful role and opportunity that you have through your teaching to improve societal conditions.

The Cultural Dimensions of Classroom Practice

The Model Alternative School Services' *Professional Development Series for Excellence in Teaching and Learning* emphasizes culturally-compatible classroom practice as the foundation for excellence in teaching and learning. The belief expressed throughout the series is that culture is integral to the actual practices in American classrooms. The approach is to make the theory and research on effective teaching, classroom management, and multicultural education more accessible and usable by connecting it in practical ways to daily classroom practice.

The four-volume series aims to have you become what Henry Giroux refers to as a transforming intellectual. A major step in the transformation is to have you begin to learn about dominant mainstream culture—something that has been omitted in multicultural discourse. The series seeks to develop your cultural and pedagogical knowledge and competence so that you can display your developing expertise in the classroom to assure learning excellence for all of your students.

The series proposes that students be taught the dominant American mainstream culture, its manifestations and ramifications, with full understanding of why they are learning it, and how they can transform and make use of this knowledge in their lives to make a difference. In other words, students learn the dominant "culture of power" thoroughly and in depth as a means to an end, so that they have essential knowledge and insight into the dominant culture, and the willingness and readiness to change "what is" toward a more embracing international culture.

The educational content, level of critical inquiry about schooling, and classroom practice strategies developed in these four volumes are not being taught in today's K-12 classrooms nor are they being taught at the university level in the schools of education. As a result of the changing face and direction of America and the void in teacher education, this professional development series is relevant, and in fact, crucial. The series is concerned with improving classroom practice on the part of beginning as well as veteran teachers. Each volume in the series is both conceptual and practical in offering original and fresh insights that are applicable in today's classroom settings.

Your Journey Through the Series

The complete MASS *Professional Development Series* gives you the basics in knowledge and skill to operate a culturally-inclusive classroom. Volume I sets the stage for improving classroom practice by providing information to develop your cultural competence and understanding of the cultural context of American classroom practice; Volume II outlines the necessary ingredients for structuring and managing a culturally-inclusive classroom; Volume III helps you design and implement a culturally-centered education program, and Volume IV presents a comprehensive model of culturally-transformative teaching for you to assure excellence in student learning.

After you complete the three modules in Volume I of the series, you should have a basic foundation and the requisite cultural competence for effective classroom practice. *Module One* offers some insights into why classroom practice that has an aim of building cultural understanding is needed. You learn, in *Module Two*, how American schools and classrooms came to be as they are as you hear the stories of the representative cultural groups who are the focus of the series: Native American, Latino American, Asian American, African American and Arab-Muslim American. Related to *Modules One* and *Two* is the perspective that you gain in *Module Three*, which enables you to examine schools and classrooms through a lens that you might not have considered before. This third module, which introduces you to critical pedagogy, calls for you to consider the contextual and historical information from *Modules One* and *Two* and your emerging knowledge of what goes on in classrooms in relationship to what you would like your own classroom to be. *Module Three* concludes Volume I, the cultural context of classroom practice.

The background you will gain in Volume I will be essential in your effort to improve classroom practice; therefore, if you choose to read only one of the books, this one should be your choice. If you choose other books or the complete series, the cultural context for the series as presented in Volume I is highly recommended for your initial study. After studying the three modules in this volume, you will surely be motivated to alter what you have been doing and apply what you have learned to more effectively embrace all of your students. For specific ways to improve classroom practice, you will benefit from studying the complete four-volume series. The three practical volumes will explain how to go about teaching to embrace all of your students. And, if you choose, you will have an opportunity to practice and further develop your cultural and pedagogical expertise through the professional development materials and personalized sessions with MASS consultants.

Volume II of the series gives you a thorough presentation of ways to employ culturally-inclusive practices as you manage the classroom. The four modules in Volume II take you from start to finish in designing and managing your classroom in culturally-compatible ways. In *Module One*, you learn how to set forth the core principles to formulate the attitudes and behaviors, which you and your students aim to work toward in your daily classroom interactions. It is these goals or standards for behavior that give direction to the management of your classroom. *Module Two* is considered to be the essential classroom management module of this volume. It helps you set up your classroom, induct your students into the classroom environment, and teach the procedures necessary to enable students to work together. Once the classroom is set up, you have the structure for orchestrating your classroom with style, sensitivity and caring. The material outlined in *Module Three* provides approaches for you to consider as you seek to build a caring classroom community. In spite of the foundation that you establish, and the way that you structure and orchestrate your classroom, however, there will be some instances in which you will need to assist students who, from time to time, may have difficulty meeting expectations and staying on course with he established core principles of the classroom community. You learn various ways to prevent and address student misbehavior in *Module Four*.

The educational program can be viewed as the substance of teaching and learning. Volume III of the series retains this viewpoint; however, it goes on further in using the educational program as a vehicle to promote cross-cultural understanding among diverse students and families. *Module One* helps you design and implement a culturally-centered education program and *Module Two* helps you connect the educational program to your work with families. A variety of methods for communicating with families and a comprehensive approach to involving families in their child's learning will be emphasized in *Module Two*.

Moving into the delivery of the curriculum, you have the opportunity in Volume IV to embrace multiple cultures through culturally-transformative teaching, a comprehensive systematic approach to precise teaching. Culturally-transformative teaching develops and refines your teaching skill, builds cross-cultural understanding, and assures excellence in student learning. The lesson framework and the teaching principles, as they are outlined in this volume, can form the basis for a complete school or district-wide teacher development and evaluation system. Your effective use of the framework and principles transforms dominant culture material and elevates your thinking and the thinking of your students.

Building cross-cultural understanding through effective classroom practice calls for you to dismantle old ways of doing things in your classroom, and to replace them with culturally compatible practices. Your ability to assure excellence in learning for all students depends on your cultural competence and commitment to operate from a foundation of cultural inclusiveness. Since American classrooms are held to a dominant culture model, you are sure to find yourself engaged in continuous examination of your belief system about classrooms, schools, and about society itself. Your professional and personal growth rests on your openness to questioning, challenging, and ultimately of changing what is to a more open and embracing educational program and environment. These professional development materials, in combination with the accompanying lectures, seminars, and personalized consultant services are dedicated to helping you become a thoughtful discerning teacher who is dedicated to improving classroom practice.

In many ways, I think of the material you are about to read as a memoir of my life as an educator. After an extended career in teaching and administration in urban, suburban, and rural schools and school districts, I have participated directly in teaching and guiding others through the experiences described in the four-volume series. These experiences have taken place in both mainstream and culturally-diverse settings and have also included consultant services in various geographical regions of the U.S. I have numerous stories to tell about my classroom experiences over a broad educational career—and this professional development series presents an opportunity to tell many of them. Some stories are more personal involving my son, who is an integral part of MASS—Model Alternative School Services—my precious and precocious nieces and other relatives that I have been honored to teach and watch blossom into caring competent adults. Others are stories about friends and colleagues whom I have been fortunate to learn from along the way, and students whom I have taught from elementary school to graduate school. My recollection of each experience has added to my understanding of schooling and of classroom practice.

Also, the research and authorities cited in the series are those whose writings I have known, loved, and lived with over time. Over the years, these "best practices" have served me well in my work in numerous classrooms from the kindergarten to university level and in professional development settings. Educators like me have respected and incorporated the concepts and principles of such noted authorities as Jerome Bruner, Jacob Kounin, Henry Giroux, John Goodlad, Grant Wiggins, Howard Gardner, and Madelyn Hunter in our classroom practices even in the face of more recent theories. These icons in the field of education didn't just give us new trends or speculative ideas—they gave us sound concepts and principles for practices that actually work in classrooms. These authors are referred to here as masters and their writings as classics because they still set the standard for the field. It was because of these and other influential educators that I was able get better and better at my craft and consequently to influence the learning and lives of my students. The topics that I have written about are referred to in this series as evidence-based, because they present clear evidence of how the concepts and principles expressed in the writing of these and other authorities actually work in practice.

I have learned from the experts, but I have also learned from active practical research in my own classroom and in numerous other classrooms from teachers with whom I have been fortunate to work and to learn from along the way. I want us to take this journey through the series together—and I want you to conclude that the series' approaches to classroom practice have been formulated in an accordance with sound evidence-based theory, research, and practices that have stood the test of time. Hopefully, you can benefit from my experience and avoid many of the trials and errors that overwhelmed me in my early days of teaching. Think of me as your mentor as I walk along side and speak to you telling my story as we go.

VOLUME I

CONTENTS

Introduction to Volume I...2

Module One

The Relationship Between Culture and Classroom Practice...7

Module Two

Classroom Practice Viewed in its Historical and Cultural Context...43

Module Three

Critical Pedagogy as a Process to Facilitate Cross-Cultural Understanding and Excellence in Learning...75

The MASS Professional Development Series in Review...104

Introduction to Volume I

The Cultural Context of Classroom Practice in American Schools

I came to an understanding of the cultural context of classroom practice through hidden doors and quite unexpectedly, or literally by accident. Throughout my educational career, which spans nearly a half-century, we have faced ongoing perceptions of school failure, accompanied by one reform after the other, and still we have not come to terms with the problem. We are still trying to figure out how to 'socialize' and teach what came to be defined as mainstream American culture to students who bring different cultural experiences and goals to the classroom—how to get them to pay attention, appreciate, and learn what the school teaches.

Arguments to explain the phenomenon of failure in schooling were put forward to suggest a lack of ability on the part of many students, notably of non-mainstream students. The students, in some instances, were labeled pejoratively as "culturally-deprived" to indicate that their learning was disproportionate to their mainstream peers. I wasn't sure what this meant at the time, but now that I am much more aware of the cultural dimension of American schooling, I have greater insight into that categorization and label. My analysis of being culturally deprived, as a state of learning or non-learning, is that for these students it was not a matter of intellect, but perhaps it was a matter of cultural deprivation, if that meant having been deprived of American mainstream culture. My further analysis of the situation more broadly is that "socialized Americans" are well-positioned to learn mainstream dominant-culture material and to perform well on dominant-culture tests because they have the requisite cultural background knowledge. *The content of American schooling is narrowly limited to absolutely reflect the dominant mainstream culture —its history and the culture of its homes and communities.*

On the other hand, one could say that the student from non-mainstream American culture who is attempting to learn mainstream culture is at considerable disadvantage—for the student is, in essence, learning a foreign culture. The implications of this for classroom practice and for learning in general are substantial. Think about the advantage for students who already know, and are steeped in American mainstream culture versus those who are learning it—many for the first time. Considering this, unless very highly motivated, these students are very likely to always be behind. School officials' creation and use of such labels as culturally deprived—or more recently, of culturally advantaged or disadvantaged—confirm that American schooling is concerned exclusively with conveying dominant American culture information, such that those who have it already are in a highly prized position of being the good students while those who don't are looked upon as the poor students. Students from non-dominant cultures have been and continue to be a monumental challenge to school officials because they often do not have the cultural background knowledge for, motivation, or stake in learning a culture or preserving a system that has little perceived relevance to them.

During the early days of my career, much of the assimilation focus had been on getting African American students to be successful in learning the curriculum of American schools while issues of integration, equity, and equality also predominated and consumed the time and attention of policy makers. Some of these issues of schooling in the desegregation era will be discussed later in this volume. Today the educational challenges of culture and diversity have been broadened to include students from multiple cultural backgrounds, and still the system of schooling has changed very little in its assimilation quest. It continues to compel all students to learn American mainstream culture exclusively with little regard for the students' prior cultural knowledge and background—an expectation that is certain to continue to thwart the level of excellence in learning for both students and teachers.

Admittedly, the process of reforming schools is complex. However, I am convinced that the quality of teaching and learning will improve if and when school policy makers choose to be candid with the American public, and with this sector of the public in particular, by openly acknowledging that *all students are required to learn American dominant culture information because…* Just this moment of truth will establish the basis for cross-cultural understanding among students and enhanced credibility for the professionals in the educational enterprise. At this point, however, there is little sign that school policy makers are even aware of the problem, nor are they willing to state the premise and rationale or even the best way to go about inculcating all students exclusively into dominant mainstream American culture.

Volume I of the *MASS, Model Alternative School Services, Professional Development Series for Excellence in Teaching and Learning* addresses this complex topic. Let me state again now as I will throughout the series, that, "Many students are unwilling to engage in an enterprise that they recognize as deceptive, and even when they do, they do so superficially for reasons other than pursuing the quality of excellence in learning that can enrich their lives." School officials, however, seem to be oblivious to the obvious in their assumption that the imposition of American mainstream culture is acceptable and accepted by the students who have to learn it.

In this volume, we will take a hard look at the system of schooling. After all, if so many students in the system are failing, isn't it time to conduct a critical analysis of the goals and means of the system itself? Should the teachers and students be blamed for failure in a system that is committed to a mission that is untenable? In this volume, you will see that the tradition and approach to operating classrooms according to dominant mainstream cultural standards to the exclusion of other viewpoints is problematic for a variety of reasons: exclusion of information, deception, and indoctrination can never be a foundation for truth and excellence in teaching and learning. Instead you will see the necessity for classrooms and practices to serve all students. You will also see the need for culturally-competent teachers who seek truth for themselves and their students and who have adopted as their mission to build bridges toward greater cross-cultural understanding as a foundation for excellence in the quality of student learning.

This volume centers on the context of American schooling, on specifically the relationship between culture and schooling in America, something that I have puzzled over much of my life both as a student and as a teacher—and which I have given considerable study and thought to in preparation for writing this professional development series. As a product of American schooling, I did not possess what I refer to throughout this series as 'cultural competence'—the knowledge, orientation, insight, or sensitivity to the issues of culture and schooling. Over much of my career, I simply did what was expected, and accepted the status quo of schooling without question. Whatever I learned about culture and schooling was on my own, often under considerable duress from the system.

Perhaps you, like me during much of my life and career, know very little about the issues associated with culture and schooling. Maybe you are also busy doing what is expected of you, giving no thought at all to such issues and even wondering why "culture" is relevant to the day-to-day practices in American schools. If you are in any of these categories, it is also important to ask whether you are aware of the adverse effect of "what goes on in schools and classrooms" on the full educational development of students, particularly of those who are outside of mainstream American culture. Without *really knowing* American schooling as it has evolved over the years, you will very likely remain in the dark and carry out classroom practices according to the same business-as-usual standard in American schooling that has prevailed for over a century.

The ability to promote cross-cultural understanding and excellence in student learning through classroom practice requires coming to terms with the ways that we all have been socialized to think about American schooling. For me, this came late in my career and only after my son, who is now a historian, presented me with information about the premise and history of American schooling that I could not deny nor refute. Once this happened, I was on the road to becoming culturally competent. I began to question and think about schooling in broader terms and to give greater attention to the "why" of what we were mandated to do in classrooms rather than simply to concentrate on "what" to do and "how" to do it. This new awareness, however, was not without pain for it was hard to reject a way of thinking and believing that over time became ingrained, colored my thinking about schooling, and defined who I was as a teacher.

The information set forth in this first volume of the series will challenge your previously held assumptions about American schools and society. Consequently, you should expect to experience temporary disequilibrium. The presentation is designed to make you more observant and open to questioning why certain practices exist in schools, to stimulate and deepen your thinking, broaden your perspective, and develop your cultural competence. Your openness to the material, and your receptivity to move outside of your immediate comfort zone to learn it, is sure to be enlightening. Through the process, you will gain new knowledge, deeper insights, and a way of thinking that will extend to your classroom and beyond.

You will be introduced, in this volume, to students from the five representative cultural groups of Americans, who will carry forth the theme and message of the series. You will also meet the group of classroom teachers who are engaged on a day-to-day basis working in culturally-diverse classrooms, who will also provide their insights in each module of the series regarding some of the issues that you may face in your classroom. The first module introduces and explains why culture and classroom practice are intertwined. In the second module, through a brief historical account of American schooling, you come to know how traditional classroom practices came to be, as well as of the plight of those originally excluded from the formation of these practices. Then, in the third module, you are called upon to analyze the current state of schooling in America. *Module Three* concludes this volume and serves as a bridge—from the conceptual to the practical. Upon completion of this module, you will have the background necessary to carry out the classroom practices in the remaining volumes of the series.

This volume, the first of the series—which provides the all-important context for American schooling—should be considered a prerequisite to the three remaining volumes of the series. Since the three classroom practice volumes are concerned with helping you to conduct your classroom with cultural competence, each will refer to and build on the cultural context developed in this volume. Therefore, this volume is essential for you to obtain the requisite background to benefit fully from learning how to employ the recommended classroom practices outlined in the remaining three volumes.

Module One

The Relationship Between Culture and Classroom Practice

Opening Scenario...8

Key Concepts...11

Topics Covered in This Module

- Why a Change in Classroom Practice is Necessary...12
- Developing a Culturally-Inclusive Mindset...13

    The Language of Culture and Classroom Practice...14

    The Importance of Cultural Competence...16

    The Limitations of Multicultural Education...18

    Teachers' Perspectives as Obstacles...21

    Adopting a World-Wide Perspective...22

- Building Your Cultural Competence and Culturally-Inclusive Mindset...23

    Learning from Real-World Scenarios: Cultural Conflict in Classroom Practice...24

    The Communication Struggles of a Latin American Student...25

    An Arab American Student Practices Customs Which Create Curiosity...26

    An Asian American Student Struggles Academically...27

A Native American Student Faces Cultural Insensitivity...27

An African American Student Responds to Hostility and Harassment...28

- Learning from Classroom Teachers: What They Think and Do...29

- Assessing Your Cultural Competence...33

- Contemplating Your Classroom Plan...34

- Setting the Stage for Culturally-Inclusive Classroom Practice...36

Classroom Teachers Talk It Over...37

A Summary of Learning in Module One...38

Opening Scenario (Afterthoughts)...39

Questions/Activities...40

Looking in Classrooms...40

Recommendations for Further Reading...41

Opening Scenario

Participants in a teacher development seminar are beginning to think about their roles in classrooms that will serve the culturally diverse students of today and tomorrow. A major purpose of the seminar is to build the cultural background knowledge of these prospective teachers as the basis for conducting their classrooms in a way that will develop cross-cultural understanding. A series of sessions is designed to enable the teachers to understand the differing backgrounds and motivations of various cultures in America—dominant cultures, immigrant cultures, and dominated cultures.

The first session is designed to encourage greater cultural awareness, to enable these teachers to understand the various student populations that will depend on them for their success. It focuses first on Native Americans—pointing out that they fall within the category of being a dominated culture because they were conquered by the government and forced to become part of American culture. The presenter of the first session introduces the participants to some of the key concepts associated with cultural diversity and explains the history of schooling for Native Americans. The session participants are eager listeners, and during the discussion phase of the session make comments such as the following:

"I didn't know there were dominated groups. I thought everyone wanted to be in America."

"I'm still not sure what you mean by building cross-cultural understanding. Are you talking about teaching us, or are you talking about how we should teach the children in our classrooms?"

"I didn't know about this history. I thought that the Indians got along with us like they did at the first Thanksgiving."

"I thought cultural understanding meant like—their foods, dances, and music—like having a festival or like celebrating everybody's culture, or something like that."

"I think if we could have learned to appreciate the land and nature from Native Americans, we wouldn't be facing so many environmental problems today."

"Now I see why Native Americans don't like the tepees and feathers that we have the kids wearing around Thanksgiving time."

"I almost feel like apologizing to Native Americans for taking away their culture."

Similar comments were made about the other cultural groups over the course of the seminar sessions, namely: Latin Americans, African Americans, Asian Americans, and Arab and Muslim Americans.

How would you describe the cultural frame of reference of these teachers? How are they like or unlike you as you begin this book? What perceptions do you have about the cultural context of schooling?
As you think about your role as a teacher in today's world of culturally diverse classrooms, you may identify with these students. How would you teach in the culturally-diverse classrooms of today and tomorrow as compared to how you might teach in classrooms serving mainstream student populations?

Understanding the relationship between culture and classroom practice is the first of the cultural competencies that Volume I undertakes so as to prepare you to conduct your classroom for building cross-cultural understanding and for promoting excellence in student learning. Your role is clear. Everywhere you look you see more and more people representing different standards of beauty, different ways of viewing the world, and different points of view about what it means to be an American. There are those who have been here from the beginning, those who arrived at different points in time over the country's history, and those who are recent arrivals. Clearly, the U.S. culture is changing simply by virtue of this new reality. It is a time of hope in a climate of change. The dominant American culture is gradually becoming less dominant, and other cultures are beginning to feel more connected and invested in what goes on in their country. The change that is taking hold in the society is naturally spilling over into the classroom. This is where the story becomes more intimate, and where your involvement comes into play.

How can you, a teacher of one of the nation's classrooms, perform your role in ways that encompass the multiple perspectives in this society? How can your classroom be a forum for influencing this society towards an appreciation of the perspectives of those who may differ from the majority view? Think of it this way. Your classroom is a microcosm of society in terms of its system of rules, expectations, and interactions. The cultural experience results from the interaction of your cultural background and the cultural backgrounds of the students that take place in concert with the school and classroom policies. In this sense, as a teacher, you are a cultural broker between your students and the classroom culture. (Freire, 1970, Giroux, 1992, Shor, 1992). Therefore, if you acknowledge these cultural backgrounds and experiences, you can create an inclusive classroom culture and build a level of cross-cultural understanding that will serve as the foundation for excellence in learning. Over time, this level of understanding will extend to the larger society as well. Let it begin with you.

In *Module One* of the series, you should focus on answering the following key questions:

- Why is a change in classroom practice necessary?

- How can you develop a mindset to build cross-cultural understanding? Explain cultural competence and multicultural education, and why a world-wide perspective is needed.

- How does the use of real-world examples help to build your cultural competence in handling the issues and challenges of classroom practice?

- How competent and ready are you to build students' cross-cultural understanding through your classroom practices?

- How can you set the stage and standard for determining growth toward a culturally-inclusive classroom so as to build cross-cultural understanding?

Key Concepts

culture ~ cultural competence ~ world-wide perspective ~ classroom practice ~ cross-cultural understanding ~ multicultural ~ multicultural education ~ cultural awareness ~ perspective ~ intercultural person ~ culturally inclusive mindset ~ empathy ~ encapsulation

Why a Change in Classroom Practice is Necessary

The question to be answered throughout this volume of the professional development series is: "To what extent should teachers be concerned with the perspectives associated with the cultural backgrounds of students in their classroom practices?" *The essential point to understand is that classroom practice is a culturally-based phenomenon centered on American mainstream culture (Giroux, 1992). What is missing is the perspective of other cultures.* Recognizing this omission, this volume explores ways to expand learning opportunities in mainstream American classrooms so as to make them culturally inclusive. This will not be easy because, to most Americans, the manner in which schools and classrooms are run has become the acceptable norm. Most teachers have grown up in these classrooms; so have their parents, and so have their parents before them. Whatever their cultural background may be, anyone who has been in America for at least a generation has experienced schooling in the "American way." Therefore, you and all American teachers have met the standard and earned membership in dominant mainstream culture—and because of this, it is sure to be as difficult for you as it was for me to see practices in schools and classrooms from any other vantage point. Yet if current practices continue, students who are not mainstream Americans will continue to be disappointed. They too wish to have their cultural backgrounds and orientations affirmed in American classrooms. And in an equally significant way, education for mainstream American students will continue to be incomplete as well. *Classrooms, as they currently exist, often unintentionally miss the opportunity to fully educate all students when they fail to recognize and to honor the values and perspectives of the many.*

When you think about it, given the assimilation mandate, the essential function of schools is to assure that students adjust to the system, and learn what the system values, and has outlined in its course of study. You and I met this assimilation standard throughout our K-12 and university level experience by not questioning, and by making adjustments to meet the requirements of the system. I am disappointed, as are many of my colleagues, that we had to wait until now to obtain a more accurate understanding of schooling in America. This story will be told in *Module Two* of this volume.

I learned personally what can result from the assimilation mandate and function of schools from my son who excelled in learning at every level in every phase of dominant-culture schooling. It was after he became a graduate student in history that he assertively began to search on his own for information that was left out of the school curriculum. Noting the omission of non-dominant culture material and perspectives only after conducting his own cultural history research was devastating, however. It severely altered his respect for the quality of education he received in American schools from kindergarten through post-graduate study.

I'm certain that uncovering such deception in the way that content is shaped in American schools is not unique. Imagine the numbers of sensitive, responsible, critical thinking students who are very likely in this same situation. Loss of faith comes when students have to find out on their own that they were not taught the complete story of events as part of their educational experience, but instead, were taught the part of the story that the establishment wanted them to know. Also imagine the number of brilliant students who actually fail in this system because they refuse to learn what they see as biased—or to be coerced in this manner irrespective of the consequences.

Knowledge, when open and inclusive, can be liberating in helping students to evolve; but when restricted and exclusive, knowledge can actually thwart the educational development of many students. If all students are to achieve their full potentials, information from all cultures and from multiple perspectives on topics needs to be taught in American classrooms. Achieving cross-cultural understanding and excellence in student learning through classroom practice requires this unbiased culturally-inclusive mindset.

Developing a Culturally-Inclusive Mindset

A culturally-inclusive mindset is the quality of being culturally-inclusive in your thinking and being—in what, and how you teach and interact in *all classrooms with dominant and non-dominant culture students alike*. It is this mindset that you must have to produce change in classroom practice. It requires you to be culturally competent, to understand the language and the issues that stem from the historical relationship between culture and classroom practice. In this section, you will learn about these ingredients and why being open to questioning traditional classroom practices is itself a cultural competence quality that you must possess in order to build the level of cross-cultural understanding that can lead to excellence in student learning. You will also see that there are beliefs in classroom practice that can limit your ability to conduct your classroom with a culturally-inclusive mindset. One limitation that seems to be unclear in the minds of many educators is the difference between multicultural education and building cross-cultural understanding through classroom practice. Another is the sincere, but limiting opposition that many classroom teachers have toward self-examination, and their consequent resistance to change. Finally, you will understand why a broader world-wide perspective is necessary and enhancing to a culturally-inclusive mindset.

The Language of Culture and Classroom Practice

A culturally-inclusive mindset calls for understanding the language, the associated terms, and the concepts that define classroom practice as a cultural phenomenon. There are several overarching questions concerning language that need to be answered. The first question deals with culture. What is culture—its significance, its components, and its application in classrooms? The second question is concerned with classroom practice. How is classroom practice related to culture? The third question has to do with relevance. Why should culture be given prominence in classroom practice?

Let's begin with *culture* and its significance. The most encompassing definition is that culture is that part of humanity's intellectual, social, technological, political, economic, moral, religious and aesthetic accomplishments. Culture is an integrated set of norms or standards—and control mechanisms—for governing behavior (Banks & Banks, 2004). Broadly speaking, culture can be conceptualized as acquired knowledge, belief systems, symbols, meanings—or whatever a person needs so as to perform in a manner that is acceptable to members of the culture. This includes the behavior, social arrangements and events, and the shared ideas and standards prevalent in a community that can generate a 'desired' social behavior. *The culture to which one belongs forms the essence or core of the person's identity. No part of the educational process is free of cultural influence.* (Pai, Adler, & Shadiow, 2006; Giroux, 1992)

Culture has been given prominence in higher education through cultural foundations courses, which are typically taken by prospective teachers as part of their teacher preparation sequence. The historical attributes of culture, usually addressed in some form in these foundations courses, will be discussed in *Module Two*. Culture, when concerned with the distinctions among cultural groups, however, is difficult to study and to apply in any meaningful way in classrooms, because the differences within and among cultures are vast. It is impossible and even unethical to pry into each student's cultural background. If we were to add to that an exploration of generational differences, mixed marriages, and socioeconomic levels, any real study of each separate cultural group would be intricate and also unnecessary in the context of this series.

My intent in this volume is not that you learn the qualities, proclivities, and nuances of each culture, in as much as this might or might not be useful for your future purposes. I do intend to have you learn about the one culture that you do know about, but might not have thought enough about—the dominant American mainstream culture, its relationship to non-dominant cultures, and its impact on the enterprise of schooling. This volume seeks to help you to understand dominant culture classroom practices in terms of their effect on both non-dominant and dominant cultures. The dominant culture perspective is that classrooms are agents for the transmission of this culture (the values, beliefs, and behavioral norms of mainstream American society) to the young. This function has become entrenched in the system. An unfortunate consequence of the culture transmission role of schooling is that it can extol the dominant culture and promote lack of respect for and appreciation of other cultures (Altenbough, 2003). In a culturally-diverse society, there are issues and needs that arise by necessity out of the relationship between dominant and non-dominant cultures. This professional development series will explore the issues and needs associated with this relationship.

Classroom practice is, in itself, a concept that needs to be understood more fully for you to have a culturally-inclusive classroom mindset. Classroom practice involves all that takes place in the classroom setting. Traditionally, classroom practice has focused exclusively on the achievement of instructional objectives (W. Doyle, 1990; Emmer & Evertson, 2009). In this view, classroom practice serves as a means to an end. Many writers suggest that day-to-day classroom practice has everything to do with how much students learn in the classroom setting. Wang, Haertel and Wahlberg (1993-94) concluded, after a half-century of research, that the way and style that the teacher conducts the classroom has the single greatest influence on student learning— greater than factors of intelligence, home environment, or socioeconomic status.

Classroom practice in this series incorporates this means-ends view, but it also considers student-teacher interactions and relationships that may occur in the contexts of all else that may be happening as desirable ends of the process as well. Classroom practice, in this series, calls also for acknowledging and shaping the classroom's hidden curriculum—a process that will be discussed more fully in *Module Three* and that will be continuing throughout the series. Shaping the hidden curriculum involves creating a classroom environment that is capable of promoting positive teacher-student and student-student interactions and relationships based on mutual respect—not only to achieve academic goals, but also to build cross-cultural relationships and understanding as the basis for excellence in academic learning.

The research also makes it clear that effective teachers are warm and caring persons who communicate respect for their students, and who have a genuine concern for their students' well-being. As a consequence of their personae, these teachers achieve positive student-teacher relationships and a sense of community in their classrooms (Hom and Battistich, 1995; Kim et al., 1995; Likona, 1991). The warm and caring ways in which teachers conduct their classrooms has a tremendous bearing on how students interact, come to respect each other, and consequently learn together. Having a culturally-inclusive mindset requires that teachers possess qualities of empathy and caring in their interactions with students.

The goals of classroom practice to build cross-cultural understanding and excellence in student learning can be achieved when you ask yourself the following question each day: "Does the way in which I am conducting my classroom (my actions or inactions) foster cross-cultural understanding or misunderstanding?" ***Cross-cultural understanding***, as it concerns the relationships between dominant and non-dominant cultures, calls for understanding and appreciating alternative world-views and multiple interpretations, ***perspectives, or frames of reference*** regarding classroom and human events. It calls for having *empathy*…walking in the shoes of the other person. Teachers who are working to achieve this status through their knowledge, understanding, and interactions are ready to progress beyond *encapsulation*—the inability to think beyond the confines of one's present culture along a continuum from *cultural awareness* (interest and observation) to *cultural competence* (having the requisite knowledge and insight) to ***cultural inclusiveness*** (operating according to an embracing world-wide perspective).

The aim of this volume is for you to reach an enlightened state of cultural awareness, so that you can become culturally competent and operate a culturally-inclusive classroom. It takes a teacher who is culturally competent—that is, one who understands the relationship between dominant and non-dominant cultures—to build cross-cultural understanding and excellence in learning through classroom practice.

The Importance of Cultural Competence

Cultural competence is essential to a culturally-inclusive mindset. But, just what is cultural competence? In a discussion about common practices in classrooms, a colleague asked me just this question regarding what I thought it might be. The manner in which she asked the question seemed to challenge my competence about the topic. I was, therefore, embarrassed and frankly insulted. She clearly got my attention, though, and I must admit that I did not know what she might have meant by cultural competence. I became introspective and began immediately to take a hard look at myself as I sought a meaningful definition. I began my actual search of attempting to decipher what it meant to be competent culturally by noting the practices that I observed in classrooms. As a result, I was able to determine what cultural competence on the part of teachers is not. For sure, competence in the sphere of culture would not be the arrogance expressed in some classrooms, which says, "The American way is the only way"…?! Certainly, cultural competence is not, I continued to reason, the common classroom practice of merely celebrating the foods, festivals, and idiosyncracies of various cultures as "sub-cultures" in relationship to dominant mainstream American culture. Moreover, "cultural competence" would not be the habit of engaging in classroom practices that unwittingly extol American patriotism and "exceptionalism" in disrespect and in disregard to the pride and status of others. After noting practices in classrooms that seemed to be harmful, and determining that these practices were not representative of the meaning of cultural competence that I was seeking, I questioned myself further. Following more reliable study and deep thought, I reached a very simple conclusion.

Cultural competence, for us as teachers, is to know and understand the relationship between dominant and non-dominant cultures and the issues associated with culture and schooling, and to know how to conduct our classrooms with a culturally-inclusive mindset. This mindset includes but extends beyond dominant mainstream American culture. The competence of having a compassionate understanding of cultural similarities and differences that we are seeking to promote in our classrooms takes on a mature form through the way that we teach and enable students to interact and to relate to each other while honoring and appreciating each other's culture and perspective. Cultural competence is demonstrated by the manner in which we teach and encourage students to challenge the assumptions of the established mainstream American curriculum and to embrace other cultural viewpoints as well. It is evident when we consciously inform students that they are learning mainstream American culture as a means to an end. In this regard, cultural competence recognizes that knowledge is power, and in view of this recognition, supports teaching students the American "culture of power" so that they can have knowledge and insight into the dominant mainstream culture as the basis for moving toward a more inclusive world-wide culture. *The important point here is that students need to be constantly reminded that what they are learning is dominant-culture material and that there are other ways of knowing and of viewing the world. Otherwise, they will assume that what and how they are mandated to learn are the only valid ways.*

Cultural competence means that we are more observant and open to questioning traditional practices in schools and in our classrooms. We have the mindset and the readiness to transcend the typical way of operating classrooms and, as a consequence, we are able to build cross-cultural understanding and excellence in student learning through our classroom practices. In essence, we have insight into the ways of the dominant American mainstream culture—the way it subtly (and sometimes not so subtly) imposes its will onto us without awakening our consciousness of the imposition. One example to illustrate the point is the phenomenon of 'time'. Time is a factor that takes different forms in different cultures. In America and in other Western-oriented cultures, time is a strongly governing factor in the lives of people. Everything runs on time…and most of us have simply accepted time in our way of doing things and do not give it a second thought.

The use of time is so ingrained in American culture that few in this culture ever stop to consider that many other cultures are not so governed by time-related factors, such as schedules, promptness, due dates, speed, etc.

There are other Western-oriented cultural factors such as *Puritan morality*, concern with thrift, self-denial, and delayed gratification; the *work-success ethic*, or achievement according to the work and the effort expended; *individualism,* concern for self, often to the exclusion of others; *achievement orientation*, continuous striving to achieve higher and higher goals; and *future-time orientation*, the look-ahead-and-plan-for-tomorrow philosophy, which are all inherent in American mainstream culture, but which may not be so strictly pronounced or featured prominently in other cultures. (Pai, Adler, & Shadiow, 2006).

This is not to suggest that this society or the school's attention to time and other Western-oriented factors should be altered drastically to accommodate those who have had a different life-orientation. It is simply to say that to be culturally competent, you should be aware of the omnipresence of such factors as time, achievement orientation, and individualism in this society and in its schools. It suggests that, in explaining the dominant/non-dominant culture relationship, you make it clear to students that the American way is not the only way to look at factors such as these. Furthermore, you should encourage empathy and respect for those who do not revere time and other commonly accepted ways of being and of doing in this way. Time, for example, is a fact of life in American schools; but when you teach students to view time and other such governing factors from multiple vantages and points of view, there is the possibility of enlightenment and growth toward cross-cultural understanding among dominant and non-dominant cultures. To the extent that the concept of time, for example, is broadened to include other perspectives, Americans too could begin to take things in stride and to relax more. Critical pedagogy, discussed later in *Module Three*, is a vehicle that can make it possible for you to engage in analysis regarding how American culture is styled in relationship to other cultures. It sets in motion a thought process that makes it possible for you to become 'culturally competent' and 'culturally inclusive' in your classroom practices.

The Limitations of Multicultural Education

Clearly, cultural competence facilitates and is essential to a culturally-inclusive mindset, but there are some limitations to attaining this mindset. One limitation is a lack of understanding about multicultural education, what it is and how it is different from building cross-cultural understanding, the relationship between dominant and non-dominant cultures—the goal of this series. Attempts to address cultural diversity in classrooms have traditionally taken form through multicultural education. Multicultural education can be characterized by equity and mutual respect among existing cultural groups (Bennett, 2007). Knowing the characteristics, interaction patterns, and approaches to learning of students from various cultures, and promoting equity and mutual respect among students are areas of interest in both multicultural education and in efforts to build cross-cultural understanding through classroom practice.

While multicultural education and efforts to build cross-cultural understanding through classroom practice are generally mutually supportive in the sense of pursuing equity and mutual respect among cultures, they are not the same, however. Multicultural education has focused primarily on the education of *students;* the effort to build cross-cultural understanding through classroom practice focuses on the *teacher*. Teachers build students' understanding of classroom events, societal norms, and each other through a cultural lens, specifically by understanding the pervasiveness and impact of the dominant American culture in relationship to other cultures.

This volume of the series is concerned with helping you gain deeper insights into the advent of dominant American culture in relation to multicultures. This will be undertaken with greater attention, depth, and historical focus in *Module Two*. At this point, it is worth noting that there has been a continuing debate throughout America's history between the advocates for schooling centered on dominant culture and the advocates of multicultural schooling. Such prominent writers as Adler (1982), Bennett (1984), Bloom (1987), and Hirsch (1987), in line with their belief that each cultural group should assimilate to a common American culture, have advocated a core curriculum centered on the historic ideals of the Anglo-American common school. On the other hand, the opposing groups, led largely by non-mainstream advocates, Banks & Banks (2004), Grant, (1992), Sleeter (1991), have proposed a multicultural approach. The debate has become more pronounced as students, separated increasingly by race and culture, have pursued equal schooling opportunities.

Multicultural education began originally as a consequence of school desegregation and of increased student diversity as an approach to address students' diverse learning needs and to help them learn to work together. It was during this period that I became intimately involved in both desegregation and multicultural education. My work as school administrator began in earnest at the height of the African American pursuit for equal schooling opportunity during the early implementation of the court cases mandating school desegregation. My work as administrator, in both urban and suburban school districts and as consultant to teachers and principals, called for me to be on the frontline responding to the needs of "mainstream" school faculties who had very little experience with "minority" students.

I learned so much about culture and schooling—and politics during this inaugural period of desegregation and multicultural education when confusion and misinformation reigned. Whether working with school faculty on administrative issues or in staff development sessions involving multicultural topics, I learned not to get lost in the details, but to stay with the "Big Picture." Often, this called for reminding school faculties that the court rulings weren't just about sending African American students to "better schools," or about having them sitting next to "better students." It was about a "bigger principle," justice and equal protection under the law—and the mandate for government schools to be non-discriminatory in its practices.

Many of the issues in staff development sessions concerned relationships, but there was also a myriad of other multicultural issues and topics. In referring to the multicultural literature as a background for our work, we found that in general the interest of "multiculturalists" was to address the socio-emotional needs of "minority" students for the purpose of building the students' self-esteem and, consequently improve their academic performance. But there were other goals, and a lack of clarity surrounded the methods as well.

John Ogbu (1992), distinguished professor of anthropology at the University of California, and James Banks (2002), the well-known theorist on multicultural education, both point out that there is no clear understanding of multicultural education. The models that have been proposed include assimilation approaches, cultural pluralism approaches, and human relations approaches. Within these approaches, the goals were to affirm the right to be different, to teach members of different cultures to respect one another, to include multiple cultures in the content of the curriculum, etc. As long as programs were diffuse, undefined, and focused on the diversity of *students,* there was general acceptance of these goals among the educational power structure. It became threatening, however, when educators were asked to address the *impact of mainstream American culture on all students, to examine their own values regarding non-mainstream students, or to make changes in the traditional ways of operating schools and classrooms.* The posture taken by the educational power structure was that multicultural education would do no harm. They saw it as a way to address low academic performance and respond to the concerns of clientele in culturally diverse settings while making few substantial changes in mainstream settings. This posture, however, was just the opposite of what was really needed.

This professional development series points out that it is those who are so steeped in mainstream culture who most need to understand and to appreciate other cultures. The dominant mainstream culture's way is so entrenched in the schools of America that it is difficult to incorporate multicultural education in classroom practice in any meaningful way. Teachers, when confronted with culturally diverse clientele or situations, may be resourceful enough to supplement what is in the textbook to include some multicultural concepts, but they are unlikely to be able to change the basic material of the curriculum. So what happens, at best, is that an Americanized version of the cultural content comes into play—and at worst, exotic foods, festivals, songs, and stories serve as the multicultural offering.

Though well intended, multicultural education in practice has been just one more way to "slice and dice" students, and one more "add-on" to the already over-crowded mainstream curriculum. All of this was just "tinkering around the margins" of the towering ubiquity of dominant mainstream American culture. The viewpoints of American educators have been so shaped by American power and dominance that multicultural education, as it has been practiced in the schools of this country, has not and cannot begin to promote the meaningful change in perception that can lead to the quality of cross-cultural understanding that is needed to promote excellence in the learning of all American students.

Teachers' Perspectives as Obstacles

Perhaps the greatest limitation to developing a culturally-inclusive mindset has been the sensitive, well-meaning teachers themselves. It has been common to hear teachers say, "I'm color blind. I treat all students the same. I'm expected to teach what is in the curriculum and celebrate our country's heroes. My 'minority' parents like the way I conduct my class. There are no 'minorities' at my school, so I have no need to be concerned with cultural diversity issues." While at the same time, non-dominant culture teachers have expressed an opposing view. They see the way that mainstream teachers work with students from other cultures as a pressing educational issue. Their view is that these teachers operate exclusively from the stance of the dominant American middle class and, as a result, foster cross-cultural misunderstanding. What these teachers see as learning and behavioral problems among many students from non-dominant cultures is often student resistance to the school's dominant-culture curriculum and classroom practices. In such an environment, the relationship between teachers and students can't help but deteriorate into conflict and discipline problems.

When reflecting on the limited perspectives of some teachers it is useful to think in broader terms. Excellence in teaching calls for teachers to think beyond the familiar, and seek new knowledge, insights, and alternative ways of thinking and viewing the world. Excellence in student learning is impossible when other cultures, other places in the world, and other perspectives on issues and topics are left out of the repertoire of teachers, and as areas of study in the school curriculum. When this happens, students receive a partial education. To be able to say, "I can broaden my horizons and competently teach students in all cultures," opens doors to a world of learning and living for both teachers and students.

Adopting a World-Wide Perspective

The limitations of the multicultural education approaches and the provincial perspectives of teachers need to be overcome. They both serve as obstacles to a culturally-inclusive mindset. Overcoming these obstacles calls for moving beyond America with its unitary nationalistic tendencies to *embrace the multiplicity of cultures in the places where they live throughout the world.* True empathy comes when cultural groups are understood *from their frames of reference*, how they think, live, and learn in their own environments. When students feel valued and understood on *their* terms, it becomes possible for classrooms to be more open, embracing, and cosmopolitan. This **world-wide perspective** requires reconciling the current local and national interests of schools with broader global interests. It requires knowing and acknowledging as valid the way different cultures throughout the world view people and events. Further, it requires all persons, mainstream and non-mainstream alike, to extend beyond their own experiences to see the interconnections of the human experience.

Fareed Zakaria (2008) suggests that power in the world is shifting and that the U.S. advantage as the lone superpower is diminishing. Therefore, out of necessity, he calls upon educators to plan for a world in which America must take its place alongside other world powers. A post-American world requires enlightened world citizens, a requirement that is within the range of development for classroom teachers. With the rise of other countries—China and India, for example—American citizens have an opportunity…in fact they have a need to extend themselves beyond U.S. boundaries to learn about the rest of the world. Education must be the bridge to cross-cultural understanding. The day-to-day practices in classrooms can be the avenue for fostering this broader world-wide perspective. U.S. citizens must take on a world-wide or global perspective and interact as citizens of the world. This requires being truly **multicultural,** able to recognize and value the distinctiveness of all cultures, and able to interact comfortably with sensitivity and respect among the peoples of the world. Bennett (2007) describes the **intercultural person** as possessing an intellectual and emotional commitment to the fundamental unity of all humans, while at the same time accepting and appreciating the differences among people of different cultures.

The world-wide perspective called for in this professional development series recognizes and values multicultural education just as it values the well-meaning intentions of teachers. It is sincerely indebted to multicultural education for the contribution it has made to understanding the complexity and challenges of culturally diverse populations living together; but unlike some multicultural approaches, which focus on students and their cultural proclivities, the aim of this series is with *you, the teacher*. The goal is to develop your cultural competence to the level necessary to conduct your classroom with cultural knowledge and insight—with a culturally inclusive mindset. In the context of classroom practice, *a world-wide perspective simply means thinking beyond the confines of U.S. boundaries to the world at large: to acknowledge, respect, and appreciate the perspectives and behavior patterns of students in their purest form, rather than through the lens of the dominant American culture.*

A culturally-inclusive mindset calls for you to understand the potentially mutually-supportive relationship between culture and classroom practice and to see cultural competence as essential to this relationship. You should know the limitations of multicultural education as a vehicle to build cross-cultural understanding and you should know the ways in which the viewpoints of classroom teachers can limit a culturally-inclusive mindset. Finally, if you are to achieve excellence in student learning, you should now know that a culturally-inclusive mindset requires you to be inclusive in your interactions and to seek to understand and teach students on *their* terms, building on *their* background knowledge.

Building Your Cultural Competence and Culturally-Inclusive Mindset

Throughout this series, you will find that what is being proposed is simply "best practice" for all classrooms. The strategies—from organizing the classroom to working with parents—are, for the most part, what would be recommended for all classrooms regardless of clientele. Cultural competence, however, asks you to go one step further. *You are called upon to recognize and consciously explain to your students that "the way we do things in the classroom" is based on dominant American mainstream culture. Further, you are asked to teach your students that—while there is the dominant and powerful American culture—it is but one culture, and not the only culture that has validity, that other cultural perspectives will be presented in the classroom in conjunction with the mainstream American culture perspective.* Cultural competence in classroom practice concerns your ability to interact effectively with both American mainstream and non-mainstream populations and classrooms. If the clientele is culturally diverse, there is a visible reason to conduct the classroom in culturally-inclusive ways. But if not, the approaches are also applicable. In fact, the recommended approaches in this professional development series are needed more, and certainly would be well received in classrooms where most if not all of the students are mainstream American. *An essential goal of this series is for you to see cultural inclusiveness as a mindset, a way of thinking and operating in all classrooms.*

Volume I, as an introduction, helps you to gain an understanding of the context and purpose of this professional development series—to develop your knowledge of the issues and possibilities associated with multiple cultures living together in a country that has been committed historically to Anglo-American culture. You will then have the necessary background to design and implement classroom practices to embrace all cultures. In this module you become aware of the issues and inherent conflict that could be obstacles in culturally diverse classrooms, but you also begin to see the possibilities for operating your classroom with a culturally-inclusive mindset and regard for cultures other than the dominant American mainstream culture. Your knowledge of many of the issues and possibilities begin in this module and extend throughout the series. One form of continuity throughout the series is to have you listen to a representative group of twelve diverse classroom practitioners who will share their thoughts about the series' concepts, principles, and practices. Another is to encourage your awareness of the issues and perspectives of students from the non-mainstream cultures most typically represented in American classrooms. In subsequent volumes, as you consider culturally compatible practices for your classroom, you are encouraged to remember and continuously hear their voices.

Learning from Real-World Scenarios:
Cultural Conflict in Classroom Practice

Imagine a student from a non-mainstream culture sitting alone in an American classroom, surrounded by self-assured mainstream American students, feeling isolated and uncomfortable among his mainstream peers. The student naturally looks to the teacher for support. But, when the teacher operates the classroom in the typical mainstream American way, the student's lack of reinforcement for his cultural background, feeling of isolation, and lack of confidence is compounded. Also, imagine how this feeling of being alone in a strange place with strange people can portray itself in such ways as poor academic performance, awkward social behavior, or even in acts of hostility.

The representative group of twelve diverse classroom practitioners was asked to provide some examples of their experiences with cultural conflict among the five cultural groups who will be represented in the professional development series: Latin American, Arab American, Asian American, Native American, and African American. The complexity of the attitudes and perspectives associated with the five cultural groups as they face degrees of conflict and discord in American classrooms are examined in the examples provided by these practitioners. You can benefit from reading their accounts. Put yourself "in the shoes" of these classroom teachers, and the students whose cultures are represented, as you anticipate the kind of incidents involving conflict between cultures that you may encounter in your classroom. As you listen to the voices in each of the scenarios, ask yourself the following questions:

(1) What do you learn about the dominant culture perspective?

(2) What role does the teacher play? Do you find it helpful or harmful?
    Please explain.

(3) What do you believe are the issues of cross-cultural misunderstanding?

(4) How would you address the issues, immediately on a short-term basis?

(5) How would you work to build cross-cultural understanding on a long term basis?

The Communication Struggles of a Latin American Student

Alejandro Garcia, a first grade Latin American student, struggles to solidify any connections in his active and fast-paced classroom. As the only student of color, he feels isolated in many of his daily endeavors. He speaks and understands little to no English, and his Spanish skills are far from efficient as well. Within his few years on this earth, his language skills have managed to become mixed and mingled, and he has not developed fluency in either language. Both Mom and Dad are Spanish speakers, and they understand very little English. You rarely interact with either parent, because they both work long hours at a local restaurant. You do notice an older sister, Maria, as she walks Alejandro to class in the mornings. You also notice her nurturing and motherly nature, and it becomes evident that she has been forced to mature far beyond her age of ten years old. Documents and forms are rarely returned, and the signature is often that of the older sister.

As the only faculty member with any Spanish background, you begin to rely on your brief two-year stint in Spanish classes in college. Communicating with the child and parent are difficult, and you find it nearly impossible to develop strategies for success. Daily, you watch Alejandro become frustrated and confused during simple instructions or procedures. He is often seen wandering around the classroom, as he tries to accomplish mundane tasks like turning in papers and lining up during transitions. You notice him watching other students intently, but he always tries to stay at a safe distance away from his peers. During instruction, he gazes around the room, and proximity does nothing to strengthen his focus. Often times, he can be seen laying his head down on his desk, and he feels most comfortable wearing a hooded sweatshirt. It is clear to you that Alejandro simply wants to hide amidst the room full of people and activity, and you desperately want to support and encourage him.

Most of the students in the class appear to pay little attention to Alejandro, but you have overheard two boys discussing their opinions of the situation. You have heard them pondering his lack of communication, and you were shocked to hear one student say, "My Mom said he's just a Mexican and should go back home." As you overhear the children, you become overwhelmingly saddened by the circumstances, and you vow to make a difference for Alejandro, your school, and your tiny rural community.

An Arab American Student Practices Customs Which Create Curiosity

Zaarak is an Arab American tenth grade student. His is a bright student, but shy—and he participates in class discussions and projects. He does well academically, but has few close friends. A few weeks into the school year, the supervisor notices that at lunch, Zaarak—who brings his lunch daily—is sitting away from the rest of the class. She asks him about his seating choice, and he replies that he wants to be quiet during lunch. She takes this as an acceptable answer, but continues to watch the lunchroom happenings. During the next several days, the supervisor notices that the other students in the class find reasons to walk by Zaarak during the lunch period, and that all of them express great interest in what he is bringing for lunch each day. Upon further questioning, the lunchroom supervisor discovers that Zaarak is observing Ramadan, based on his religious belief. Ramadan is a Muslim religious observance that takes place during the ninth month of the Islamic calendar, believed to be the month in which the Qur'an was revealed to the angel, Gabriel, to deliver it to Prophet Muhammad. It is the Islamic month of fasting, in which participating Muslims do not eat or drink anything from dawn until sunset. Fasting is meant to teach the person patience, sacrifice, and humility.

In order to teach Zaarak about fasting and the importance of Ramadan, his mother packs him only two pieces of bread and a bottle of water for lunch each day, along with his copy of the Qur'an, which he is expected to read from daily. He complies with this, since the rest of his family gets no food at all during the day. The other students, not understanding the reason behind his small lunch, begin to speculate and spread rumors about Zaarak's home and family life. The rumors include everything from his family being too poor to buy food, to his parents refusing to feed him because he has bad behavior. All of these rumors are hurtful to Zaarak, who feels ashamed to talk to his teacher about them. So, he ostracizes himself from the group, unwittingly drawing even more attention.

An Asian American Student Struggles Academically

Jihye is an eighth grade Korean American student. Although Asian American students have a reputation in the school of having positive attitudes toward education and of doing extremely well academically, Jihye struggles in many areas. Even though she has advised her teacher that she does not understand many concepts, the teacher overlooks this by saying that she is being modest and doesn't want the other students to know her intellectual ability. Jihye is becoming extremely frustrated and is starting to act out in class. She is very distracted and unfocused during instructional periods. Jihye is also distracting other students by engaging them in conversation while the teacher is explaining important concepts. Jihye has not turned in her homework for the past week and her explanation continues to be that she does not understand what to do. The teacher consulted Jihye's parents, but they too are at a loss for understanding that Jihye has difficulties, because all their other children have excelled in academics. The other students have picked up on the fact that the teacher thinks that Jiyhe is more intelligent than they are, and they are either ignoring her or making rude remarks to her. This is also causing Jihye to withdraw from interacting with the other students.

A Native American Student Faces Cultural Insensitivity

Shyann is a second grader who has recently moved from an Indian reservation in Wyoming. So far, her transition has gone well. The biggest difference that Shyann has noticed is the food being served in the cafeteria, and that the color of her skin doesn't match any of the other students. Many students in her classroom have been curious about where she has come from, and interested in the ways and customs she has that are different from theirs. Her teacher, Mrs. Applegreen has been impressed with how smart she is and surprised by her eagerness to learn. She has observed only a couple of incidents where Shyann has not seemed happy with her new school and classmates.

On the first day, some of the children greeted her by saying, "How!" to which Shyann responded, "How what?" with an angry face. On the playground one day, a student asked her if she was a squaw. This made Shyann cry. Other than that, Mrs. Applegreen feels she is "fitting in" well.

The other day, while discussing decorations for the upcoming fall festival and first Thanksgiving Feast, the teacher announced that the second grade would be in charge of making dream catchers and headdresses with feathers. She was sure that this would be a great way for the children in the classroom to get to know more about Shyann's heritage, and a way the class could honor her culture.

When Shyann heard about all of the plans for the festival and feast, she began to cry and say she would not do it. The teacher was surprised at her unwillingness to participate and at her ungratefulness. After all, these plans were meant to celebrate Shyann. After class, the teacher asked Shyann to stay in from recess to talk about what had happened. Through many tears and coaxing, Mrs. Applegreen learned that the reason she did not want to participate in the activities was because it would be wrong. Shyann explained that using feathers would be wrong, because they are very special and only to be used in very important ceremonies. She said that dream catchers are sacred to her people and the children in her class won't know or understand what they are for.

An African American Student Responds to Hostility and Harassment

Mynique Williams' family moved to a town just outside of Atlanta, Georgia in the middle of the school year and enrolled in a local elementary school in a predominantly white neighborhood school. The principal placed Mynique in a fourth grade classroom, where she was the only African American student. Throughout the day, the teacher, Miss Nichols, would find Mynique sitting alone crying while rocking back and forth at her desk. Finally, Miss Nichols goes up to Mynique and insists that she tell her why she is behaving in this manner. As a result of Miss Nichols attention, Mynique's behavior begins to worsen and it continues to deteriorate, off and on, over a course of three or four months.

Then, one day Mynique complains to Miss Nichols saying, "They call me Brillo Head."

Miss Nichols responds by taking Mynique aside and when she asks her who is calling her this name, she refuses to talk about it.

A week later, Mynique is seen near the bathroom striking a little boy in the nose. When Miss Nichols intervenes, Mynique says, "He picked on me and I tried to ignore him, but I couldn't hold it in any longer."

The accused student denies ever picking on Mynique and his fellow classmates side with and agree with him.

The next day, Mynique's parents come to school to complain about the students and the demeaning incidents that are happening with increasing frequency at the school. They want the teacher to do something about the continuous harassment of their child.

Miss Nichols decided to discuss it with the principal before proceeding. The principal's advice was, "Well, if you didn't see it, it didn't happen. It will blow over."

It all came to a head when, a few days later during seatwork activities, Mynique turns over a desk, screams, points to a group of students in the class and says, "They called me a 'nigger' and told me I would never have friends because I am black."

The teacher runs over to restrain Mynique—and even though she did not witness the events that Mynique had described, she decides to call the parents of the identified students.

The parents refuse to take any responsibility. In fact, one parent tells you, "It's not my fault that a little black girl has been placed in my son's class."

How did you handle each of the scenarios involving students from a non-mainstream culture attempting to interact in a typical classroom of mainstream students?

The representative group of classroom practitioners report that *multicultural and multiracial conflict presents the most difficult of their classroom problems.* Some classroom teachers consider such conflict as crises requiring disciplinary action, and some feel that simply talking it over with the individuals involved is sufficient. The scenarios reveal that there are no simple or easy answers. Each requires careful analysis, thought, and sensitivity and could be symptomatic of the teachers' cultural competence or lack thereof. Each scenario presents a classroom dilemma to which the solution may not be readily apparent. The dilemmas in each are an opportunity for you to begin to think about classroom issues and possibilities, and then plan to be proactive with the hope of avoiding the conflict that they present. Your plan for preventing misunderstanding should be to operate your classroom in ways that build cross-cultural understanding through your classroom practices.

Learning from Classroom Teachers: What They Think and Do

The diverse group of twelve classroom practitioners was also asked in an interview to take an in-depth look into the inner workings of their own classrooms. The interview focused on the readiness of these practicing classroom teachers to build cross-cultural understanding in their classrooms in several areas:

(1) What do they know about the backgrounds of various cultural groups in America?

(2) What thoughts do they have about what goes on in their classrooms that could inhibit cross-cultural understanding and excellence in student learning?

(3) What do they believe teachers can do to promote cross-cultural understanding and excellence in student learning through their classroom practices?

<u>Some of the responses they gave to the question of knowing the background of various cultural groups were:</u>

"When considering the backgrounds of various cultural groups in America, I find myself not entirely knowledgeable of the subject. I do know that America is based on European beliefs. I don't know much at all about the background of other cultures."

"I never would have thought about culture as being important in how I conduct my classroom. It didn't seem relevant to me."

"I never learned anything about cultural groups in America in any of my high school or college classes. I never had any courses in multicultural education and therefore I have very little background on the subject."

"As a teacher, I think it is important to seek an understanding of cultures world-wide but I don't know much at this point."

"Honestly I just never paid much attention to having a background in the foundation of American schools even though I believe that it could help me understand schools and work better with other cultures today."

"I hate to admit it, but I had never thought about anyone else's background except my own. I just took it for granted that everyone thought the same way about schools that I do. This is the way we all learned to think"

"I don't know much right now but I am eager to learn."

To the question concerning what most inhibits cross-cultural understanding and excellence in student learning in their classrooms, some of the responses were:

"My problem is that I don't know much about other cultures, but I am learning. My progress has been gradual involving many observations, experiences and interactions with other cultures in the classroom, on the playground, with parents and with peers."

"To gain cross-cultural understanding takes moving beyond the comfort of the known, beyond the mainstream and being open to new ways and ideas, but this is hard to do."

A number of insightful responses were shared to the request for ways to build cross-cultural understanding and excellence in student learning through classroom practices:

"I never thought very much about the practices in my classroom. I have been so busy just trying to do everything that I am asked to do. There's just no time to think very much about anything else."

"When you do things pretty much the same way every day year after year, you just don't think about it; it's kind of like automatic."

"I know that some of the things that I do in my classroom might be troubling to some people but I am required to teach American holidays such as Columbus Day, Independence Day, and Thanksgiving."

"Some of the ways that I work with students from other cultures may not be the best because I don't really know them as well as I do my other students, but I do as well as I can."

"Religion is a touchy subject, but I believe that if I could talk more about what people believe and how this affects people's attitudes and actions, they would be more accepting of others."

"When it comes to embracing other cultures, the only thing I can think of is our annual international night where each grade level is assigned a country to represent and provide a sample of their food."

What then is the proper method for assessing the extent of teacher competence in creating a culturally-inclusive classroom? We believe that how students live together, learn together, and play together under our direction are the indicators of cultural competence. This professional development series helps you become an informed culturally competent professional who is able to conduct your classroom with skill and sensitivity—with a culturally-inclusive mindset. The interviews of the twelve representative classroom practitioners, however, reveal that there is minimal readiness among these practitioners, and very likely among teachers in many American classrooms, to effectively handle sensitive classroom situations. Yet today more than ever, society needs teachers who are international and empathetic in their interactions with others, and who are truly committed to excellence in student learning. These teachers possess the cultural competence to develop knowledgeable citizens who will also be committed to cultural inclusiveness and cross-cultural understanding.

Assessing Your Cultural Competence

How ready are you to begin the task of carrying out practices in your classroom to build cross-cultural understanding and excellence in student learning? Your responses to the following questions will help you organize your thinking in preparation for study in this professional development series. Before moving on, please assess your current level of cultural competence as you begin your study. Use the scale below each item to respond to the following questions:

1. How much do you believe that you know about the history of schooling in America—or, how schools came to be as they are?

    A lot　　　　　　　　　Some　　　　　　　　　Not much

2. How much do you know about the history and education of the five representative cultural groups who are now in America's schools?

    A lot　　　　　　　　　Some　　　　　　　　　Not much

3. To what extent have you thought about or taken the time to analyze what goes on in classrooms from the perspective of non-dominant culture students?

    A lot　　　　　　　　　Some　　　　　　　　　Not much

4. How aware are you of the "Culture of Power," the way the dominant American culture plays out in schools and society?

    A lot　　　　　　　　　Some　　　　　　　　　Not much

5. What do you know about the "hidden curriculum" and its function in classroom practice?

    A lot　　　　　　　　　Some　　　　　　　　　Not much

6. To what extent have you thought about the ways in which the development of standards for student behavior and interaction in your classroom can be broadened to include all cultures?

    A lot　　　　　　　　　Some　　　　　　　　　Not much

7. To what extent have you considered strategies to structure your classroom to make it an organized, welcoming environment for all students?

    A lot　　　　　　　　　Some　　　　　　　　　Not much

8. How prepared are you to orchestrate a culturally-diverse classroom and build a community of caring?

    A lot　　　　　　　　　Some　　　　　　　　　Not much

9.	How prepared are you to develop a comprehensive (fair, appropriate, and consistent) policy and plan to address student misbehavior?		
	A lot	Some	Not much
10.	To what extent have you considered strategies to address cultural diversity as you implement the curriculum?		
	A lot	Some	Not much
11.	To what extent have you begun to formulate teaching strategies that would embrace all cultures?		
	A lot	Some	Not much
12.	How comfortable are you working with culturally diverse families?		
	A lot	Some	Not much

Your answers to these questions will help you assess your learning needs and guide you in planning your study in this and subsequent modules in the professional development series. You are not expected to have well-formulated answers to these questions as you begin your journey toward creating a culturally-inclusive classroom. You will, however, be able to answer each question, progressively, as you proceed through this volume, and assuredly, should you complete the course of study outlined in the remaining volumes in the series.

Contemplating Your Classroom Plan

Teaching a classroom of twenty-five or more students over a nine-month school year requires considerable thought, planning, implementation, reflection, and follow-through. Whether you are a prospective teacher or a currently practicing teacher, there is so much to think about and accomplish. To ensure that your classroom practices are thoughtful, consistent, and predictable, you need to have a plan—a road map—of what needs to be done, when it needs to be done, and how it needs to be done. As you engage in this professional development series, you can use this as an opportunity to prepare a foundation for your own classroom plan in two ways:

You can use the material to develop a thoughtful classroom philosophy, incorporating the contextual background and critical pedagogy reasoning set forth in the three modules of this volume.

Relationship Between Culture and Classroom Practice

Historical Insights

Critical Pedagogy

You should take great care to compose and articulate your philosophy statement in writing. The philosophy statement should explain how your classroom would depart from the traditional way of operating classrooms toward operating it in ways that build cultural understanding and excellence in student learning.

You can provide the highlights of the topics identified below. Give your explanation of how you will address the topics in your classroom.

Behavior Standards—Core Principles

Classroom Structure

Classroom Orchestration

Handling Misbehavior

Educational Program
Working with Families

Culturally-Transformative Teaching

One module in the series is devoted to each topic. The module associated with the topic discusses the major understandings, tasks, and strategies that you will need to include in your classroom plan. As a result of the knowledge gained from your study of the module, you can then explain how you will apply your newly acquired knowledge and insights in your own classroom.

Upon completion of Volume I, it is recommended that your philosophy be developed as a statement to reflect your developing cultural competence. As you study each module, it is recommended that you add to your plan. If you complete all modules in the series, your classroom plan can then be complete.

You may be a teacher in a traditional self-contained classroom at the elementary level or typical departmentalized classroom at the secondary level. In either case, there are some common strategies, applicable to all classrooms. You will have the opportunity to learn about the commonalities and address the uniqueness of your classroom situation in your plan.

The development of your classroom plan will result in a plan of action for you to use in your teaching. If you are already teaching, you can assess where you are in terms of operating a culturally-inclusive classroom, and develop a plan of action to make appropriate changes in your classroom's operation. In either case, as you see how the plan works in the classroom, you can continue to refine and use it from year to year as a ready reference and guide to growth in your classroom practices. In essence, your classroom plan can be your essential professional growth plan.

Setting the Stage for Culturally-Inclusive Classroom Practice

Volume I gives you the necessary background for the series. In this volume you begin to develop your cultural competence so that in the remaining modules, you will have the essential background knowledge and culturally-inclusive mindset to conduct your classroom in ways that build cross-cultural understanding and excellence in learning. The basic premise of the series is set forth in the following statement:

Education in a universal context considers the rich diversity of humans as a treasure to be cherished and protected. Culturally-competent teachers seek to provide students with the tools to achieve excellence in learning, and they actively search out and encourage students to seek global knowledge and perspectives. They model openness and flexibility as important attributes of cultural inclusiveness. Teachers, themselves, are open to growth and change, and they encourage their students to become change makers.

Students are affirmed for their diverse cultural heritages and experiences. Each student is made to feel important, appreciated, safe, secure, and wanted as an important member of the class and not susceptible to disregard, sarcasm, or other painful tactics. Practice begins in the classroom to give students world-knowledge, skills, and voices that add power to their impact outside of the classroom.

If your day-to-day classroom practices are in keeping with this premise, you are building the level of cross-cultural understanding that is essential to achieving excellence in student learning. This statement recognizes that the practices you employ in your classroom are all-encompassing. They include the content and process of teaching and other day-to-day practices that you and every classroom teacher must perform. Everything that you do from the way that you arrange your classroom, the environment, materials, and overall atmosphere that you establish through your interactions with students should be done with a culturally-inclusive mindset.

It should be comforting to know that the knowledge you gain in this series will make it possible for you to conduct your classroom effectively, at the outset, as you begin your teaching. You will also have the tools to analyze your growth in building cross-cultural understanding and excellence in student learning throughout your career. This four-volume series offers you all of this and more.

To conclude this module, the diverse group of twelve classroom management practitioners, introduced earlier, was asked to give their understanding culture in classroom practice as developed in the first module of Volume. They responded accordingly:

Classroom Teachers Talk It Over

"I have been trying to understand the difference between cultural competence and cross-cultural understanding in classroom practice. Now I understand it to be that cultural competence is what the teacher has to have in order to work with students to build cross-cultural understanding and excellence in student learning."

"Isn't multicultural education and cultural understanding still somewhat the same? I think you should know as much as possible about the students' cultural backgrounds to build cultural understanding in the classroom. Still, there is so much to know about each different culture that it would be hard to do."

"I really know American mainstream culture since I live it every day, but I hadn't thought about what it means to know about mainstream American culture in relation to other cultures."

"Today, when the world is a global village, it is important to know about the cultures of the world. That means you need to be well informed in order to inform the students. By having the correct background knowledge about American and other world cultures, you, as a teacher are raising the bar for your student's own cultural understanding and excellence in learning."

As you conclude this module and other modules in the series, consider the views of these teachers and be prepared to give your view? How do your thoughts compare with the views expressed by these classroom practitioners?

A Summary of Learning in Module One

This module has been designed to give you an introduction to the world of cultural diversity and its relationship to classroom practice as the introduction to the remaining modules of the professional development series. Its major purpose has been to give you an overview of what it means to build cross-cultural understanding and excellence in teaching and learning through classroom practice. It has provided the background to help you conduct your classroom in culturally-inclusive ways. In review, some specific points are:

- The module has focused on explaining the reason why classroom practice and cross-cultural understanding are combined in this series and the opportunity that you have as a classroom teacher to build cross-cultural understanding and excellence in student learning through the way that you conduct your classroom.

- The module has explained what is necessary to have a culturally-inclusive classroom mindset. The language associated with cultural diversity is explained in detail. Cultural competence is highlighted because of its significance in classroom practice for building cross-cultural understanding. Multicultural education and classroom practice combine in a complimentary and distinctively useful way to build cross-cultural understanding. Multicultural education is concerned more with students and their learning while building cross-cultural understanding is more concerned with you, the teacher, and your competence in conducting your classroom. A world-wide perspective is needed to obtain the perspectives of other cultures on their terms rather than through the lens of the dominant culture.

- The cultural conflict examples among students from the five representative cultural groups in the series depict situations that you are likely to face in your classroom. The scenarios illustrate the intricacy and delicacy of some of the issues. From the examples, you can see that there is much to consider that may not be readily apparent on the surface. You are encouraged to be proactive by effectively conducting your classroom to embrace cultural diversity. But, then, if such conflict arises, you should probe deeper for the underlying causes of such conflict in relationship to your overall classroom approach.

- You have also been introduced to a diverse group of practitioners who are currently working in the classroom on a daily basis. They have shared their understanding of classroom practice and cross-cultural understanding. They will continue to share their thoughts about the content of each module with you. The

- viewpoints, issues, and questions that they raise should be helpful as a comparison with your own developing knowledge as you go through the various modules of the series.

- At this point in your development, you should be at some point on the continuum of being more culturally aware—culturally sensitive—culturally competent. Remember, more than being a level that you attain, cultural competence is an attitude and growth process. Your current assessment of competence and readiness to build cross-cultural understanding and excellence in student learning through your classroom practices can be your barometer as you learn more in each module of the professional development series.

- Initial information has been provided to help you consider a plan for your classroom. The information and recommendations in this module help you contemplate your classroom plan. Your plan can develop over your course of study in this professional development series. Volume I helps you to formulate your philosophy statement and the remaining volumes in the series will help you design the classroom practices for your plan.

- The establishment of a guiding/mission statement to direct your classroom practice efforts is important. Your mission statement can accompany your philosophy statement as part of your classroom plan. The sample in this module can be helpful to you in assessing your growing ability to build cross-cultural understanding and excellence in student learning through your classroom practices.

This module has concentrated on giving you an explanation of the role that classroom practice can play in building the level of cross-cultural understanding that ensures excellence in student learning. Now that you have looked closely at the ideas presented, you should be able to see that what is being proposed is simply high-quality, *effective classroom practice*. Cultural enlightenment in considering the practices that you employ in your classroom has been the goal of this module. In the next module you will learn the role that a study of history can have in the influencing your cultural knowledge.

Opening Scenario (Afterthoughts)

How would you describe your cultural frame of reference after studying the material in Module One? Please give examples to explain some specific insights that have gained from the module.

Questions/Activities

The following questions, exercises, and activities will help you assess your level of cultural competence upon completion of *Module One*.

1. Explain the rationale for a world-wide perspective to developing cross-cultural understanding and its necessity in classroom practice.

3. Explain the following concepts in relationship to your development as a culturally competent classroom teacher:

   Culture   classroom practice
   Culturally inclusive mindset   universal view/perspective
   Cultural competence

4. From your previous analysis of the five cultural conflict examples, discuss the classroom practice issues? The cultural conflict issues? What approaches would you use in your classroom to address the issues in ways that get at the underlying causes of the conflict?

   Cooperative Group Activity:

   Based on your assessment earlier in this module, explain your background and readiness to conduct your classroom in a culturally inclusive way. What areas of study seem most relevant and necessary for you as a classroom teacher? Discuss in small groups. Then explain in the large group session.

Looking in Classrooms

Visit a school in your area to find out the extent to which the classroom teachers seek to build cross-cultural understanding through their classroom practices. Observe and note the following. *(Ask questions of the teachers in areas where you need clarification)*:

1. In what ways is American mainstream culture depicted in the classrooms? And, to what extent are the teachers aware of this representation?

2. In what ways are the classrooms culturally inclusive? Explain.

3. Do you notice anything that violates the principle of cultural competence? Explain.

Then, write a brief <u>Descriptive Summary Statement</u> to explain what culturally relevant practices you observed in this setting in relationship to what you would do in your own classroom.

Recommendations for Further Reading

Bennett, C. I. *Comprehensive Multicultural Education,* 6th ed. Boston: Pearson Education, 2007.

    Bennett provides a comprehensive overview of the issues associated with cultural diversity. It is a wonderful resource for educators to obtain an introduction to the field.

Gay, G. "Multicultural Teacher Education for the 21st Century." *Teacher Educator,* (2000) 36 (1), 1-16.

    Gay presents a strong argument for teacher education programs that prepare European Americans to teach ethnically diverse students of color.

Ming, K. and C. Dukes. "Fostering Cultural Competence through School-Based Routines." *Multicultural Education* (Fall 2006) 14, (1), 42-49.

    Ming and Dukes make the link between cultural competence and classroom management while placing an emphasis on developing cultural competence.

Zakaria, Fareed. *The Post-American World.* New York: W.W. Norton & Company, 2008.

    This book calls upon Americans to prepare for a world in which American power will give way to the rise of other powerful nations in the world. The book makes the case for a stronger emphasis on the world's cultures in American schools.

Module Two

Classroom Practice Viewed in its Historical and Cultural Context

Opening Scenario...44

Key Concepts...47

Topics Covered in This Module:

- How History Influences and Develops Your Cultural Competence...48

- Cultural History Context and Insights...49

    Your Family History and Cultural Background...49

    The Language and Manifestations of Cultural History...51

- A Historical Overview of Anglo American Culture and Its Dominance in American Schools and Society...53

- Selected Highlights of Five Cultural Groups in American Classrooms...57

    The Schooling and Conversion of Native American Cultural Groups...57

    The Schooling and Americanization of Latin American Cultural Groups...58

    The Complex History and Struggle for Schooling and Civil Rights of African American Cultural Groups...60

    The Education and Socialization of Asian American Cultural Groups...62

    Obtaining Cultural Awareness and Understanding of Arab and Muslim-American Cultural Groups...64

- Contemporary Manifestations of the Dominant Culture's Power in American Schools and Society…66

Classroom Teachers Talk It Over…69

Summary of Learning in Module Two…70

Opening Scenario (Afterthoughts)…71

Questions/Activities…71

Looking in Classrooms…72

Recommendations for Further Reading…72

Opening Scenario

Kelli Morgan is a sensitive conscientious teacher of history at Danville High School in the heart of a northern U.S. city. She has taught history courses to students from a broad range of cultural groups at all high school levels—freshman, sophomore, juniors and seniors. After several years of teaching, she began to ask herself, "Why is there such a lack of interest, apathy, and occasional hostility expressed among so many of the students in my classes?"

Determined to get at the root causes of the apparent disinterest which often resulted in discipline problems among her students, she began to take a closer look at the curriculum, the textbooks that she uses, and her teaching of the material. She also began to think about the cultural make up of her classes, something she had not done before, because she had been taught to believe that teachers should not be concerned with the cultural or racial backgrounds of their classes for fear of being biased. She was taught that all students should be treated the same.

She felt that it was necessary this time, however, to look at all things that could be having an impact on her students' behavior and learning. And, as she began to think back, she could recall some of the questions and challenges she received from some of the "minority" students at points in time as she got into some areas that they believed were inaccurate.

Her content analysis of what she teaches, and her reflections on the way that she teaches, revealed that she was teaching a preponderance of U.S. history courses compared to courses focusing on other parts of the world. She also discovered that the textbooks described historical events through the eyes of the government rather than through the eyes of the people who lived the history, and that there were omissions and distortions about the selected topics for study. For example, in one of the adopted U.S. history textbooks, there was less than two pages devoted to slavery, a half page devoted to the "Trail of Tears," and even less devoted to the Japanese internment during World War II. Moreover, the presentation of this history seemed slanted to convey the courage and heroism of the country's leaders.

Even though, she was teaching the prescribed curriculum, it seemed to her that something was amiss. She thought again about the broad array of students sitting in her classes and tried to put herself in their shoes as she taught a history that seemed mostly concerned with fostering pride and patriotism toward America and nothing about their lives and interests. She had recollections of each of the students' faces, and realized that for some of the students, the history she had been teaching was not entirely accurate. Then she became concerned, "What about their history?" She was saddened, though, when she realized that she knew very little about *this* history.

What do you believe are the issues in this scenario? Describe the perspective of the curriculum planners, the teacher's perspectives, the students' perspectives. As you prepare to become or continue your role as a teacher in today's world of culturally diverse classrooms, how would you approach a similar teaching scenario? How do you think this history should be taught?

Knowing the history of American schools and classrooms is the second of the professional development series' cultural competencies to serve as context and preparation for you to conduct your classroom to develop students' cross-cultural understanding and excellence in learning. From your study in Module One you could see the relationship between culture and classroom practice, why the two are inseparable and should be studied together. This module adds to your understanding by increasing your knowledge of culture and its influence in the history of schooling in America. There are multiple stories to tell, many that are not commonly known in K-12 schooling, about the ways in which traditional classroom practices have evolved in this country.

As expressed earlier, I really became disillusioned when presented with American history information that was more credible than the information I received in American public schools. This reality was very disturbing for it caused me to be doubtful of everything else that I had been taught. Both the practicing and prospective teachers in my university classes also came face-to-face with the advocacy and patriotic function of American history and the realization that they too were given only part of the history of schooling in America. They also viewed the omission of information and patriotic presentation of their study of history in K-12 classrooms as untenable in light of their later analysis of reality. To reiterate, nothing can be more damaging than to have those who have trusted so completely in the education system of this country come to terms with its selective content and story line, omissions, and distortions. The result is a loss of confidence and trust in the system.

This module seeks to reveal the storyline and some of the omissions and distortions. The stories about schooling for culturally dominant mainstream Americans in contrast to schooling for non-dominant cultures, can promote cultural awareness which in turn can begin to change the way you view American schooling. This module is basic because it provides the necessary historical background for you to formulate a culturally inclusive approach to classroom practice. Clearly, your cultural knowledge and ability to effectively carry out the classroom tasks of later modules will be limited without this background.

As you study this module, you should focus on answering the following key questions:

- How does a study of history influence and develop your cultural competence?

- What is the context of cultural history, your cultural history and background and the language surrounding cultural history? Explain their influences on your perspective today?

- What features of the history of Anglo-American culture are dominant in American schools and society?

- What features of the history of the five major non-western cultural groups are omitted and or distorted in today's schools?

- What are the dominant culture issues that continue to restrict cross-cultural understanding in today's schools? Explain the influences of language and the biases teachers may hold as a result of their education and socialization in American schools and society?

Key Concepts

dominant American mainstream culture ~ cultural assimilation ~ involuntary/ dominated cultures ~ ethnocentrism ~ cultural supremacy ~ voluntary/immigrant cultures ~ manifest destiny ~ melting pot ~ culture of color ~ nationalism ~ minority group ~ cultural imperialism ~ cultural inversion ~ prejudice ~ ethnic discrimination mainstream values ~ racism ~ race ~ stereotyping ~ acculturative ~ enculturative

How History Influences and Develops Your Cultural Competence

History is a way of finding out how the world came to be as it is. Without history we are without foundation, without memory, and without explanations. *If we who do not know history—our own and the history of this and other societies—we cannot understand life in America in relationship to the rest of the world.* The study of history makes us more intelligent. We need the content of history, what happened when. Even more, we need the historical thinking that comes with being aware of the bigger picture surrounding issues and events, and the habits of mind that promote thoughtful reflection and analysis.

In this module, you learn about issues associated with public schooling that you might not have studied in your high school or college history courses. From your schooling in American classrooms, you very likely learned about history and schooling from the perspective of mainstream American culture. You surely learned about the country's presidents and other American patriots and heroes. On the other hand, you probably learned little about why public schools were established and how these early schools influenced the way schools and classrooms operate today. Like most Americans, you very likely have been so thoroughly socialized in the dominant American culture as the way of life for everyone, that it may to be difficult to visualize or understand the perspectives of others who are not so socialized. How much do you know about the level and quality of education of non-mainstream Americans and about other circumstances that directly impact their socioeconomic status? How much have you thought about the perspectives they may have about American schools today and why? Here you will obtain a brief overview of the history of dominant mainstream culture and some of the historical highlights of five of the other cultural groups that are now part of American classrooms—Native Americans, Asian Americans, Latin Americans, Arab/Muslim Americans, and African Americans.

Most Americans arrived here from someplace else in the world at various times during the history of the country, and for various reasons. Some groups faced a few obstacles, others faced more, and still others faced many. Often there has been a direct relationship between the hardships faced by the group, its educational status, and its consequent social and economic mobility in American society. Each group of Americans has depended upon the educational system to be the means of setting the group on the road to the "good life" in America. And for each, the good life has meant learning the rules of mainstream America.

Cultural competence and a culturally-inclusive mindset are essential to classroom practice to build cross-cultural understanding and excellence in student learning. Throughout our careers as educators, we will meet and attempt to influence students from multiple backgrounds. We, therefore, need to be seen as competent and credible by all students, for many students are unlikely to fit into what has become the typical classroom model. Having culturally diverse students in the classroom gives us a special opportunity to do more than simply organize and operate a smoothly-running classroom. After studying this module, however, you will realize that *even if you don't have a culturally diverse classroom, the source of needed change resides within traditional mainstream classrooms. With this realization, there is a need for you to build your knowledge and the cultural background knowledge of all students that you teach.* From the historical knowledge that you will obtain in this module, your educational development as a culturally competent classroom teacher will be greatly enhanced. This level of knowledge and openness to other cultures begins by being introspective and looking into your own cultural background.

Cultural History Context and Insights

The historical study of the various cultural groups described in this module will be more meaningful to you if you begin by looking at yourself within a world-culture context by taking a look at your background and that of your family, in relationship to the dominant mainstream culture of the United States. In this regard, this book is experiential in asking you to become a part of the process. Since the focus of this part of the series is to develop your cultural competence, it is appropriate for you to do your own historical research to learn about your family history and involvement in schooling in America.

Your Family History and Cultural Background

Clearly, there was a substantial population of Americans on this continent before the history that we recognize began. Your family may be among this population. Or, as with most Americans, your family may have arrived in America from some other place in the world. In either case, you should begin your historical research by going back as far as you can in your family's history and describe the events that surround your family's first contact with America. Your historical research should focus on where your family came from, why, and the effect of education on your family's development and status in America today. Use the following questions as your guide but add other information that may contribute to your cultural background knowledge:

1. In what part of the world did your family reside before coming to the US? Why did your family come to the United States?

2. In what approximate year did your family arrive in the United States? What difficulties did members of your family face as a consequence of their arrival?

3. What schooling opportunities were available to your family members upon their arrival in the United States and over the years since their arrival in America?

4. What kind of schooling opportunities do you believe have been available to families from other cultural groups over the historical period of your families' arrival in America? Provide a rationale for your belief.

5. How much is your cultural group represented in the educational program, the textbooks, the cultural celebrations, and in determining the standards of success in the schools of America?

6. How much are groups other than your cultural group represented in the educational program, the textbooks, the cultural celebrations, and in determining the standards of success of the schools of America?

7. What is your socioeconomic status in America today and what do attribute it to?

8. What perceptions do you have about the schooling that you received in K-12 American classrooms? Explain in detail why.

9. What perceptions do you have about the schooling that other cultural groups have received in American classrooms? Explain in detail why.

10. What changes regarding cultural diversity would you like to see in K-16 American schools?

After you know the history and distinctions that characterize other cultural groups in relationship to your cultural history, you can obtain a more complete understanding of the significance of culture in today's schools and classrooms. Your own direct personal experience can create empathy and help you think and feel deeply about the issues involved. This in turn makes it possible for you to extend your perspective and approach to embrace other cultures to gain cultural competence. Cultural competence, after all, is as much a way of thinking and feeling as it is knowledge and skill. Your own cultural history can be a reference point as you become familiar with the language that has evolved, study the history of American schools in general, and get to know the history of the various cultural groups in the remainder of this module.

It is important that you keep in mind, though, that just as your history and experiences are personal and deeply held, history for others is also personal and deeply held. For example, to lump individuals in each of the groups: African Americans, Native Americans, Asian Americans, Arab Americans, and Latin Americans together into one group, could be viewed as *stereotyping* them by making broad generalizations to describe all members of the group. A simplified view of culture and over-generalization of cultural characteristics in any respect is limiting and can lead to erroneous and even harmful judgments. A person characterized as Asian, could be a native-born American, an immigrant from Laos, Thailand or Cambodia, Vietnam, the Philippines, or Japan. The person may or may not speak the same, or have much in common with others categorized as Asian. *Knowledge of culture can give only general clues, insights, or explanations for a person's behavior or attitude.* Nonetheless, because people become individuals through their culture, it is important for classroom teachers to become conversant with and empathic toward multiple cultures as a prerequisite to being effective in a 21st Century classroom.

The Language and Manifestations of Cultural History

Different cultures encourage the performance of certain tasks and the development of certain qualities in their members to deal with the circumstances they face in a particular society. Therefore, since the cultures of the five groups depicted in this module have evolved from the historical circumstances they faced en route to the United States to the present time, the categories of dominant, dominated, and immigrant cultures are appropriately descriptive. The *dominant mainstream culture* is the prevailing Anglo-American culture. *Involuntary or dominated cultures* are those who are here because of slavery or conquest, and oppression by the dominant culture. Among these groups are African Americans, Native Americans, and some Mexican and Puerto-Rican Americans who became part of the United States through conquest. *Voluntary or immigrant cultures*, on the other hand, are the first generation of groups who freely chose to come to America.

These distinctions in language are very significant because they have everything to do with the perspectives, motivations, and attitudes of cultural groups today and the way different cultures deal with the circumstances they face in a society that is governed by the dominant mainstream culture. When you look at this phenomenon historically, it is easy to see why members of dominated cultures who did not choose to be here might have perspectives, motivations, and attitudes that differ substantially from members of immigrant cultures who chose freely to be here. To act without this knowledge is to operate in the dark without a key piece of information. It should be noted, however, that the dominant culture as it has evolved over time is not merely an Anglo-American or

White American phenomenon. As I pointed out earlier, anyone who has been educated in American schools has been influenced by, and has earned membership in the dominant American culture. This includes most if not all American educators regardless of race or national origin.

The term *culture of color*, is now used to depict many in these five cultural groups because they tend to have a darker hue to their skin color. This description is considered less offensive and more descriptive than *minority group* or *minorities*, which implies lesser status than the dominant or majority group. Still, even in many of today's schools where African and Latin Americans predominate the term minority is still used to classify cultures of color. All of this has a bearing on the way that culture interacts with schooling in America.

Education in the United States is not only *enculturative*, as when a student from the mainstream culture learns about his or her own culture, it is also *acculturative*, as when a student from a non-mainstream cultural group learns about mainstream culture, a new and different culture. The point was made in Module One that the student from non-mainstream culture who is attempting to learn mainstream culture is learning a foreign culture.

Classroom teachers typically have given little thought to the history of American schools and why classrooms operate as they do. This is where understanding the establishment of American schools by a segment of ***European Americans***, specifically the Anglo American founders, who set forth the habits, values, behaviors that formed the core of American schooling is significant. This group of Anglo Americans and those who followed in their footsteps are referred to in this series as the dominant American cultural group since they tended to think of and define themselves as the "norm" and others who sought to retain the customs and views of their nation of origin as *ethnic* or minority.

The American dominant culture is based on this group of European Americans' view of the way things are to be done, often referred to as ***middle class norms or mainstream values***. Consequently, non-dominant cultural groups whose motivations, talents and interests may be at odds with the norms and values of the dominant culture, may have degrees of hostility toward mainstream institutions and little respect for, or willingness to participate in, what they see as an oppressive system. They may be inclined toward ***Cultural inversion***, which some dominated cultures have adopted. Through cultural inversion these dominated cultural groups have alternative views and regard certain mainstream American behavior, events, symbols, and meanings as inappropriate for them.

America and *American* are used generally and in this book series as well to define the United States and its citizens. The abbreviation, U.S. is also used for convenience. It should be understood, however, that when America or American are used interchangeably in this narrow way, these categories are inaccurate and offensive to other Americans. The terms are inaccurate because America covers the entire Western Hemisphere and the terms are offensive because their use typically does not embrace all of the citizens of North, Central, and South America.

Much of the history of schooling in America has concerned the quest for *cultural supremacy*, the domination of a Protestant Anglo-American culture in the United States. It was the belief of the Anglo-European colonists in their superiority over other cultures that caused them to engage in policies and practices designed to eliminate and subjugate cultures they believed to be of lesser quality and status. Common schools were set up by and for this "superior culture" to perpetuate Anglo-American values.

A Historical Overview of Anglo American Culture and Its Dominance in American Schools and Society

In this section, you will become acquainted with the history of schooling designed by Anglo Americans, for Anglo Americans, in the interest of Anglo Americans. Critical to your understanding of how schools and classrooms took on the role of enculturation and acculturation to the dominant culture is to understand the historical events surrounding the development of the common school.

After the Revolutionary War, the diverse backgrounds of European Americans along with Native Americans and African Americans posed major questions for the leaders of the newly created United States government. Of the questions, there were three that are most associated with the direction taken in American schools and classrooms. One question was, "Would it be possible for a diverse multicultural society to survive or was the survival of the nation dependent upon a single unified culture?" A second question that was of major significance to these early leaders was, "How can we have freedom and still have order?" And, the third question was, "What type of knowledge would be needed by an educated citizen? Governmental leaders pondered these questions and concluded that there would be (1) a national culture based on Anglo-American ideals, (2) freedom controlled through the inculcation of Christian values, and (3) a nationalistic political belief system controlled by creating an emotional bond of patriotic loyalty between citizen and government. The schools and classrooms of the nation through their practices were designated to serve as the agencies to achieve these goals: to ensure perpetuation of a society centered on Anglo-American ideals, Christian moral values, and nationalism to promote and extend American power.

Government leaders plan for the schools and classrooms of the nation to ensure the enculturation/acculturation of citizens to the protestant Anglo-American culture has been realized in many respects, but there have been periods in the history of public schooling in America when this function of schools has been challenged. In the <u>Troubled Crusade: American Education, 1945-1980</u>, Diane Ravitch (1983) addressed the role of schools in this manner:

> Defined as they were so often as instruments of national purpose, educational institutions have become focal points for large areas of consensus… but they also served as magnets for dissension, attracting all those who wanted to change the social order…. (Ravitch 1983, xxii)

This consensus and challenge began with the inception of the common school and continued throughout the 20th Century as part of the common—public school connection. With the first goal of centering schools on American ideals, at least partially accomplished, it can be instructive to contemplate for a moment the second goal, which concerned achieving freedom with order, Christian moral values, and the role of religion. Lawrence Cremin (1970) captured the sentiment and overriding function of religion as the basis for the moral values which the founders wanted when he wrote the following:

> When the Puritans settled in the Massachusetts Bay Colony in the 1630's, they believed they were creating a model religious community. Early Puritan Leader, John Winthrop told his fellow colonists in 1630, "We must consider that we shall be as a city upon a hill, the eyes of all people are upon us." Their goal was to create …a well-ordered religious society…. (Cremin 1970, 12)

The third goal involved the knowledge needed by the educated citizen and dealt with the question of whether the curriculum should deal with the processes of learning such as reading, writing, and thinking and let citizens form their own political beliefs as proposed by Thomas Jefferson, or whether the governmental institution should define the content of what was to be learned. It is important to look more deeply into this question, for the decision was made in favor of government control. In fact, one could say the approach to schooling was to be all encompassing designed to promote loyalty and love of country by creating an emotional connection to the symbols of America. The promotion of loyalty included Americanization programs such as teaching history, language, literature, and songs to reflect nationalism, flying and pledging to the flag, and performing patriotic exercises.

A predominant figure in this nationalistic movement was Noah Webster, often called the American schoolmaster. Webster believed that moral values should be imposed. And, like the early settlers of New England, he equated moral values with Protestant Christian morality. He was a prolific writer, who promoted patriotism and fostered a national culture through the nationalistic themes of his spelling book and his standardized dictionary of the English language. These patriotic teachings, he believed, would produce a citizen eager to serve in the armed forces and increase dedication to the causes of government. During the time of World War I, the pledge of Allegiance, the singing of patriotic songs, and other patriotic exercises as well as an emphasis on school spirit, became an inherent part of the American classroom. By taking on this role of fostering patriotism and nationalism, schools and classrooms were at the forefront of promoting what would become the major source of cultural domination and war throughout the 20th century to the beginning of the twenty-first century.

The belief of these early government leaders was that the process of socialization through the schools was to be dependent upon the way the classrooms were operated. The groundwork was laid for how classrooms should operate by controlling the learning environment through discipline, orderliness, cooperation, and obedience. This belief was set forth in the way classrooms were structured and managed and the materials that were used. For example, moral character was developed through the school's use of student books such as the popular McGuffey readers, and William Bagley's widely used book, <u>Classroom Management</u>, was used to control the environment. The practices within classrooms were to be the methods for inculcating governmental values.

At the approach of the twentieth century, immigrant populations increased dramatically and secondary schools were faced with unemployable immigrant adolescents, seeking a better life. As students became more diverse the purpose of education was redefined and tracking was adopted to prepare these young people for their places in society. Even though a monolithic view of schooling was pursued, tracking, which called for assigning students according to their ability, to separate academic or vocational tracks within the school, promised something for everyone, but not the same thing for everyone. This approach to schooling was seen by some as the "new equality."

The schools met varying degrees of success in achieving the three goals outlined by these early government leaders. Horace Mann, while working toward instilling a common political view through the schools of the nation, gained his reputation as

America's greatest educational leader. He wanted all students to attend the common, same type of school, so that all would have the same education. However, Mann's dream of having students from different backgrounds attending the same school and classroom failed to be realized. Instead, a variety of schools in different settings—suburban, private, and urban—have developed to accommodate students from differing social backgrounds. Racially segregated communities and schools continue to be perpetuated and some students receive an education that is qualitatively different from others. Mann also believed that by fostering shared political beliefs and avoiding controversial topics, the survival of the United States government would be ensured. Moreover, he believed that without such a belief system, American society would be doomed to political strife and chaos.

Mann considered the school to be the key to moral and social development. The classrooms of the nation, he believed, should teach and instill moral values in students; that is, the moral values common to the Protestant religion. However, in the effort to promote social development, the school has taken on more responsibility than perhaps it should have. The family and church have been replaced by the school in promoting society's values. For example, character education, drug abuse, and sex education have increasingly become a part of the school's curriculum. There has clearly been a long and complex history of schools' involvement in social improvement. And, despite the school's dismal record of success in these areas, society still turns to the school and classroom teacher to handle society's social problems.

From this brief summary, you have a thumb nail sketch of the historical background of public schooling in the United States. The approach has been pervasive and enduring and certainly not neutral as many have supposed. As a classroom teacher, you need to be consciously aware that the dominant culture in the United States which stems primarily from Anglo and Western European traditions, has largely determined the mainstream culture's official language, moral values, and institutions. People, who are part of this culture, have learned to see reality in similar ways, and have developed similar ways of thinking, valuing and believing, and of determining what is "good" or "bad." You have been introduced to the source of this "mainstream" culture, its traditions and manifestations in schools and classrooms. Now you will also find out about other cultures with different histories, perspectives, and traditions.

Selected Highlights of Five Cultural Groups in American Classrooms

Many classroom teachers have never considered the various circumstances under which cultural groups other than the dominant culture came to this country and the ways in which an understanding of these circumstances might affect the perceptions these cultural groups have about what goes on in American classrooms today. Consequently, selected highlights of the history of Native Americans, Latin Americans, African Americans, Asian Americans, and Arab/Muslim Americans are presented from the frame of reference of each group. Howard Zinn (2003) in his book, <u>The Peoples' History of the United States</u>, emphasizes the importance of finding the future by learning the hidden history of the people who lived it when he proposed the following:

> If history is to…anticipate a possible future without denying the past, it should, I believe, emphasize new possibilities by disclosing those hidden episodes of the past…. (p. 11)

Only when you understand cultural groups from their perspectives through the lens of its history can you obtain the background necessary to begin to walk in the shoes of the broad array of people who are in the United States of America today. Each group has a legitimate story to tell and that is what this module hopes to accomplish, to have you, who are to serve as classroom teachers for the schools of the country *really listen to each of the groups* who have played a part in this country's development and who have significant roles to play both in the schools, and in directing the country's future. Of course, it is impossible to adequately tell the story of each group in the context of this volume. Because of this limitation, many of the concepts are general and could lead to misunderstanding. Nevertheless, this module provides a glimpse into the historical backgrounds of the five cultural groups, who represent dominated and immigrant cultures and the role that government, including the school system, played in their history.

The Schooling and Conversion of Native American Cultural Groups

<u>Native American</u> as opposed to American Indian is used in this series to recognize the indigenous nations in the Western Hemisphere as the original inhabitants of this land. The term Indian recalls Columbus's way of naming the people that he found. Here, the preference is to use Native American to denote the original inhabitants, the Americans who are native to this region. At the same time, the series recognizes that in many other respects, Native Americans, like the other cultural groups to be examined in this volume, are very different from each other.

Soon after their arrival in this land, the colonists attempted to destroy the language and culture of Native American tribes. It was from the deception and slaughter of conquest, and the Naturalization law of 1790 which denied them citizenship, to the struggle for civil rights in the 1950's and 1960's, that Native Americans have felt the pain and suffering of the dominant American culture. Joel Spring (2005) in his book, <u>The American School</u>, captured the prevailing sentiment:

> Attitudes of cultural and racial superiority underpinned plans for the religious and cultural conversion of Native Americans. English colonists brought with them a sense of righteousness about their protestant beliefs and the superiority of English culture. Colonists branded Native Americans as "heathen savages." (p. 23)

In 1819, Thomas McKenney, head of the department of Indian Affairs, convinced Congress to pass the Civilization Fund Act, which funded Christian Missionaries to educate Native Americans. Thomas McKenney expressed to the Native American people that the key to their success would be for the government to establish religious schools so that they could share in the "glory" of Christianity and Anglo-Saxon culture.

The Indian Peace Commission Report of 1868 emphasized that language differences were a major source of conflict between Native Americans and Whites. The teaching of English was adopted after this report was released under the premise that by speaking the same language, there would be greater similarity of thought and sentiment between Indians and Whites. This similarity would then make the assimilation of Native Americans into the broader culture more likely. Boarding schools for their early education were also adopted because officials believed it was important for Native American children to be removed from their family and tribal influences. Much has been written about the treatment of Native American children in these boarding schools, but for purposes here, it is significant to note that it was because of these schools that Native Americans began to demand control of their children's education and the restoration of their language and cultural heritage. The right of Native Americans to operate their own schools was finally made possible through the principles embodied in the Indian Self-Determination Act of 1975 through 1988.

The Schooling and Americanization of Latin American Cultural Groups

The terms ***Hispanic and Latino or Latina*** have similar connotations. Latin Americans may or may not share a common language and the same cultural values. They may have come from a variety of countries including Mexico, Puerto Rico, Peru, or Guatemala to name a few and, therefore, broad generalizations can lead to misunderstanding. Many Latin Americans in the U.S. are descendants of Mexican people who lived in what is now the Southwest and became Americans not of their own choice but as a result of the spoils of war. Almost all other Latin Americans migrated here from the other Americas. As a group, Latin Americans are a mixture of European, American Indian, and African cultures. When considering the motivations and attitudes of Hispanic (which invokes the historical relationship of Spain with this group) or of Latin American groups more broadly again, it was the attitude of racial and cultural superiority professed by early European Americans which Joel Spring (2005) referred to as prevalent in subjugating this cultural group:

> The attitude of racial, religious, and cultural superiority provided motivation for the United States to take over Mexican land, fueled hostilities between the two countries throughout the nineteenth and early twentieth centuries, and it was reflected in the treatment of Mexicans who remained in California and the Southwest after the U.S. conquest and of later Mexican immigrants. Segregated schools, housing, and discrimination in employment became the Mexican American heritage. (p. 171)

In 1848, the treaty of Guadalupe Hidalgo, which ended the Mexican American War, resulted in disaster for Mexico. In this treaty, Mexico lost almost half of its total territory while the United States gained major parts of what would become the states of California, Colorado, New Mexico, Nevada, Arizona, Utah, and Texas. Thus, hostility between the two countries prevailed throughout the 19th and 20th centuries. This hostility was reflected in the attitudes of the Mexicans who remained after the United States conquest and of later Mexican immigrants who were lured to the U.S. to become farm laborers. Even though citizenship was granted by the treaty, severe limitations were placed on voting rights, access to housing, public accommodations, and schooling resulting from whether Mexican Americans were to be considered Caucasian or Indian. Of great concern to the conquered Mexican population was the attempt to eradicate their Spanish language and the mandate that English was to be taught and used as the language of instruction. This concern continues today.

A similar fate befell Puerto Rican Americans when this cultural group became a United States colony at the end of the Spanish American War in 1898. The policy was to gain the loyalty of a conquered people by using education as an instrument for Americanization. United States educational policy called for replacing Spanish with English and for introducing children to the dominant U.S. culture through such practices as pledging to the U.S. flag, studying important historical figures, celebrating U.S.

patriotic holidays, and attempting to replace their curriculum, textbooks and teachers with those who represented the American way of life. The battles are still being fought today among these groups, who reflect a combination of both dominated and immigrant cultures trying to make a way for themselves in United States public schools.

Most Cubans came to the United States after Fidel Castro overthrew the Batista's dictatorship in 1959. They were political refugees who felt threatened and sought freedom and security in the U.S. rather than the prosperity sought by most immigrant groups. In fact, those who came during the U.S. government airlift between 1965 and 1973 tended to be from the upper and middle class. Most were admitted to the U.S. without waiting for visas or other restrictions. The 1980 Mariel boatlift immigrants were less well-off and not as well received. Today there are close to a million Cubans in the United States. More than half settled in Florida; others settled in places like New York City or Los Angeles.

The Complex History and Struggle for Schooling and Civil Rights of African American Cultural Groups

African American, the classification used most often today to describe this group of Americans, is used in this series. The classification, African American, has undergone multiple transformations from negro with a small "n" to denote the dominant culture's lack of recognition and respect for this cultural group immediately after slavery, to the era in which it was given greater status and thus capitalized as Negro. Other categories have included Coloreds or Colored People or from Black People to simply Blacks depending upon the historical period and who was writing the script. Then there was the hyphenated form Afro-American as part of the movement for self-determination. African American is another umbrella term used for a wide range of people who seem to share some of the same values, physical characteristics, economic levels, political and religious views, but often have little in common. Perhaps no other cultural group can recount as much complexity in its history as African Americans. Spanning several centuries, the history of African Americans can be viewed as having occurred in three periods: The first was slavery beginning with capture in Africa and close to 300 years of bondage; the second, emancipation and another nearly 100 years of sharecropping and further exploitation; and the third, another move toward freedom which occurred through the northern migration and Civil Rights movement.

In the first period between 1502 and 1860 over 400,000 Africans had been forced into slavery in North America and by 1860 the population had grown to more than 4 million. Slaves, who were the personal property of their masters, were in absolute bondage for life and denied rights to property and all other legal and civil rights including the right to receive an education. The extent of government power in African American enslavement is captured by Eugene Genovese (1972) in his highly recommended seminal book on the depth of chattel slavery, or slaves as property, from the slaves' perspectives, <u>Roll Jordan Roll: The World the Slaves Made</u>:

> The laws of Virginia and Maryland, as well as those of the colonies to the south, increasingly gave masters the widest possible power over the slaves and also, through prohibition of interracial marriage and the general restriction of slave status to nonwhites, codified and simultaneously preached white supremacy. Thus, the master class, for its own purposes wrote chattel slavery, the caste system, and color prejudice into American custom and law. (p. 31)

The second period was characterized by sharecropping and the drive for self-determination. The decade of reconstruction immediately following the Civil War ushered in a period of hope for African Americans. African Americans gained political and civil rights through the Reconstruction Act of 1867 and the 14th and 15th Amendments, but it was the rejection of proposals for land distribution, that trapped them into a system that took two world wars and the New Deal to bring about its demise. So, while African Americans were no longer slaves, they became sharecroppers who worked the land of their former masters. Thus, a period of extreme degradation and discrimination continued to be the fate of this group of Americans.

The third period, which took place during the first half of the 20th century, was characterized by African Americans moving north to seek a better life in the cities of America. Nicholas Lemann (1991) reflected on the pride that has enabled African Americans to surmount their difficulties in his book, <u>The Promised Land: The Great Migration and How It Changed America</u>:

> In black Chicago....the South side had plenty of slums—the worst slums in Chicago, physically—but it was the seat of civilization, the home of the great black institutions of the middle class. Like Harlem, it was a place whose name connoted pride and the possibility of success all over black America. (p. 81)

African Americans faced hardships and many were ill prepared for what they would find up north. It is generally agreed, however, that this period of urbanization led to the destruction of racial segregation in the South and to the Civil Rights Movement of the 1950's and 1960's.

Lawrence Levine (1977) helps us put the complex history of African Americans and its impact in context. In his scholarly book, <u>Black Culture and Black Consciousness</u> he gave us an all-encompassing description of the complex nature of African American thought and style as it developed during slavery:

> The essence of their thought, their world view, their culture, owed much to Africa, but it was not purely African; it was indelibly influenced by the more than two hundred years of contact with whites on American soil, but it was not the product of abject surrender of all previous cultural standards in favor of embracing those of the white master. This syncretic blend...of the African and the Euro-American resulted in a style which in its totality was uniquely the slaves' own and defined their expressive culture and their world view at the time of emancipation. (Levine 1977, 135)

African Americans have made great strides in equality since the days of slavery and are beginning to see a future beyond this history.

The Education and Socialization of Asian American Cultural Groups

Asian Americans include a number of diverse groups. Among the groups are: Chinese, Japanese, Filipino, Vietnamese, Korean, Pakistani, and Indian Americans who differ in history, culture and language. Most Asian Americans freely chose to immigrate to the United States, and as a result, have a strong desire to become exemplary U.S. citizens, to learn English, and other cultural behaviors which exemplify the American standard. They are the fastest growing cultural group estimated to reach 6.4 percent of the U.S. population by the mid-twenty-first century. In 1970 the Japanese formed the largest group, surpassed by the Chinese in 1980.

The Chinese were hired to work on the transcontinental railroad because whites during this period were more interested in seeking gold in the western mountains. The Chinese Exclusion Act had a devastating impact on the Chinese American community. With its passage, Chinese Americans were denied the right to become naturalized Americans.

The Japanese came later, as Joel Spring (2005) recounted:

> Although California employers saw Japan as a cheap source of Asian labor, anti-Asian hysteria greeted the Japanese as it had the

> Chinese. While native whites worried about job competition and the resulting low wages, Japanese entered the country with expectations of becoming permanent citizens with high educational standards. The Japanese, like the Chinese, were caught between American companies wanting to use cheap oriental labor and American workers who did not want the competition. (p. 182)

Since the end of the wars in Vietnam, Laos, and Cambodia, Southeast Asians and Filipinos have come to the United States. Included among the most recent immigrants were heterogeneous groups from Southeast Asia, ranging from the well-educated families and leaders from South Vietnam, to the destitute boat people and largely non-literate mountain tribesmen like the Hmong and Mieu from Vietnam and Laos. Many were refugees of war and almost half were school-age children. The first group of immigrants included many who were professional wealthy, well-educated members of the elite who had relatively high economic status in their own country and had been exposed to English and Western culture.

Asian Americans have felt instances of prejudice as part of the socialization process. Perhaps the greatest example occurred after December 7, 1941, when the Japanese bombed Pearl Harbor. President Roosevelt then ordered the relocation of many Japanese, even those who were native-born United States citizens, to concentration camps.

Though once called the "yellow peril," Japanese Americans are now often stereotyped as model minorities. Yet many people do not realize the struggles the Asian culture had to endure to become part of the United States. The success of Japanese Americans in American schools has been proclaimed as the "bootstraps" example which other nonwhites, namely African and Mexican Americans should emulate.

Because of the choice that they made to come to the United States and their similarity of values and aspirations to mainstream Americans, Asian Americans were highly motivated to participate fully with the dominant culture in American institutions, including the schools. The Buddhist-Confucian ethic of hard work has contributed to their success in the United States. They have the highest literacy rate among ethnic groups and they tend to be well off financially. In many circles, they have been given the distinction of being "just like whites." The diversity of Asian Americans, has offered this group a wide-range of experiences and varying degrees of success both in American schools and in American society.

Obtaining Cultural Awareness and Understanding of Arab and Muslim American Cultural Groups

The designation Arab American and Muslim American are the classifications perhaps most in need of clarification. ***Arab Americans*** share a common background with the Middle East and North Africa, whereas ***Muslim Americans***, like Jewish Americans derive a sense of community from their religion rather than race or nation of origin. Muslims come from a variety of ethnic, linguistic and cultural backgrounds. Arab Americans also are from different countries with different allegiances and interests.

Culture, language, and religion have contributed to uniting Arabs toward a common perspective. It is not appropriate, however, to equate being Muslim with being Arab or vice versa even though there is considerable overlap between the two cultures. The largest Muslim countries are not in Arab parts of the world. And, even though the immigrant Arab community in the United States shares a common ethnic background with the Middle East and North Africa, an Arab can be Muslim, Christian, Jew or another belief. Nevertheless, the Arabic language has attained high status as the language of all Arab countries because the Qur'an was written in Arabic.

Religion, rather than race or national origin, has been the source of identity for both the indigenous African American Muslims and the immigrant Muslims. Muslims believe in one God who is Allah, that Mohammed is his prophet and messenger, and that they are to recite the Qur'an in Arabic. Consequently, Arabic-Islamic schools have developed wherever large numbers of Muslims are concentrated. Though Muslims feel strongly about Islam, Judaism, and Christianity being part of the Abrahamic tradition, they have felt excluded as members of this religious tradition.

The Arab American Community is now estimated to be over two million and is considered to be one of the fastest growing immigrant groups, settling all over the United States, especially in New York, Chicago, Detroit and Los Angeles. Arab American culture is complex. As Egyptians, Palestinians, and Iraqis, with each coming from different countries, they tend to congregate and support the interests of their country of origin. Cultural, linguistic, and religious affiliations serve as a unifying force. And, the persistent Arab-Israeli conflict contributes to a growing sense of identity among Arab Americans.

Muslims have felt considerable discomfort and prejudice against their religion and way of life, especially with what they believe to be unbalanced and prejudicial media coverage and references to them as "fanatic Muslim fundamentalists." Similarly, they feel restricted in their freedom to dress according to custom, to attend Friday prayers, and not to conform to other American customs like dating and free mixing between the sexes.

Without a doubt, the cultural groups discussed in this section have faced hostility in the United States environment and in their classroom environments as well. The descriptions of the groups who are now the most prevalent in United States' schools have suggested that the extent to which a cultural group has allegiance to the way of life in America and to the schools which perpetuate this way of life has largely been dependent upon whether the group *chose or was coerced* into being here. The groups most likely to "fit in" have been those who wanted to leave their homelands and who therefore made great sacrifices to obtain what they perceived to be the "good life" in America. Those less likely to "fit in" have been those who were forced to be in this country against their will.

The histories of the five cultural groups are all different and contrast with the histories of European Americans discussed earlier. This history of American schools has rarely been told in educational textbooks. Consequently, most classroom teachers know little about the source and influence of dominant mainstream American culture. They also know little about non-dominant cultures and, consequently, lump together the immigrant cultural groups who made the *choice* to come to America with the dominated cultural groups who were *forced* to be in America. This misunderstanding persists and is a major impediment to cross-cultural understanding. The result is that classroom teachers operate under the inaccurate assumption that everyone regardless of historical and cultural circumstance is committed to and eager to learn whatever it takes to be socialized into American society.

The history of dominant and non-dominant cultures provides critical insights that are crucial to becoming a culturally competent classroom teacher. After studying these historical accounts, your classroom planning can now occur with a full understanding of the formation of these early dominant-culture schools and of those who were excluded from these schools. The question you must now answer is how students from multiple cultures will coexist in your classroom, an American classroom that stems from these early schools.

Contemporary Manifestations of the Dominant Mainstream Culture's Power in American Schools and Society

As a result of this history and its impact on the interactions of dominant and non-dominant cultural groups in American schools, there are contemporary manifestations which you should be aware of in your role as classroom teacher. One of these is *race*, which is a social construction used to group humans according to observable traits such as skin color and hair texture. Race is particularly significant because it has become a legal term and has been cited in major court cases involving African Americans. Culture, on the other hand, is a construct which can be learned and modified over time. Broken down further, there are culturally-derived terms which are of major interest to classroom teachers for they under gird the basic philosophy of American schooling. ***Cultural assimilation***, calls for cultural groups to give up their original culture and become absorbed into the dominant culture. Cultural assimilation has been associated with the idea of ***melting pot***, which overlooks cultural differences and seeks to have culturally diverse students educated in "the American way." Other concepts stem from the history, goals, and purposes of dominant-culture schooling. ***Ethnocentrism***, another concept closely associated with culture as it has taken form in American schools, is a belief in the superiority of dominant culture as seen in the westward expansion's effect on Native Americans and Latin Americans. This led to the notion of ***manifest destiny***, the policy of expansion which compelled the dominant cultural group in America to view as inevitable its supreme right to spread its ideology across the nation and world. A similar state of ethnocentrism takes the form of ***nationalism***, exalting ones' own nation above others, as seen during times of war. Ethnocentrism can also have the effect of ***cultural imperialism*** which others are compelled to adopt the norms of the dominant culture and reject the culturally distinctive patterns that have served them well.

Ethnocentrism, manifest destiny, nationalism, and cultural imperialism, which paint America in a negative light, are concepts which the dominant culture would prefer erasing from the American lexicon. And even though most textbooks avoid discussing them, this professional development series would be remiss if it failed to take a look at the reality of American expansionism in terms of its impact on cross-cultural understanding. Classroom interactions are constrained when prejudice, stereotypes, and discrimination exist and they often take form when facts are omitted or fabricated and as a consequence, truth is hidden. ***Prejudice*** is an enduring attitude toward a race of people based on preconceived judgments or beliefs that develop from faulty information. ***Discrimination*** is the overt expression of prejudice. ***Racism*** is a complex concept based on attitudes of racial superiority and institutional power which involves systematic oppression of a supposedly inferior race of people. These concepts have developed as a result of the dominant culture's perceived superior status in relationship to other cultural groups. Throughout the history of America in general, and schooling in particular, there has been this interplay of such forces and reactions. Many classroom teachers are at a loss for ways to deal with the language and the insecurities they may experience in coming to terms with this history.

Marx and Pennington (Marx and Pennington 2003) sought to openly address the dominance of mainstream culture and associated issues by focusing on the position of advantage held by mainstream classroom teachers and the perceptions they may have as a result of their socialization in mainstream American society. The researchers addressed but sought to move beyond the usual feelings of insecurity and guilt and instead to focus on having the teachers learn about the history of oppression and its contemporary manifestations in the schools. Their thesis was that, "although contemporary times are frequently considered an era of 'colorblindness,' a country such as the United States with a history enmeshed in slavery and segregation, cannot truly practice colorblindness" (Marx and Pennington 2003, 93).

The researchers studied student interns in a predominantly Latin American school. They wanted to establish ways to have the prospective teachers involved in the study begin to talk about the manifestations of the dominant culture. This, they believed would move the interns to a more critical, more empowered understanding of the dominant culture and its influence in American education. In an attempt to open the door to such understanding among the student interns involved in the study, one of the researchers engaged in self-disclosure and began to reveal her personal experiences to the students:

> I have taught children of color for more than a decade. I am a white teacher. Race is a topic I have heard brought up by educators, school administrators, and university professors many times, yet the word "Whiteness" has been mentioned in only a few of my university graduate courses. Whiteness as a social construction, as a way of understanding the world and the world of schools, was rarely discussed....I recall learning about other cultures and how to teach "them" but my culture and its influences on education and my teaching was never addressed. (Marx and Pennington 2003, p.93)

Some very interesting and applicable insights about issues of power between teachers and students emanated from the research of Marx and Pennington. Some students in the study became vividly aware of their power and privilege as members of the dominant mainstream society. For these student interns, their power and privilege created a duality. They learned that while they were in a position to make crucial decisions about the schooling and futures of their students, they found that they could not communicate effectively with the students or their parents. They could move in circles of comfort outside the classroom; yet, they found that they were unable to manage the students in their classrooms. Thus, they lived with the two-sided perspective of being powerful and powerless.

The most salient finding from the study was that the participants who admitted their privileged position in the dominant culture of power and took responsibility for it, developed a belief in their ability to be effective in their classrooms. These participants developed the critical consciousness—the power to transform reality. Initially, the student interns believed that their role in this predominantly Latin American school was to *teach the dominant culture to their students*. They found, during the course of the study, to look closely at their own status and come to terms with the dominant culture and its impact on them and their students.

The researchers related that most educators consider the topic of "Whiteness," as often folded into the dominant culture paradigm, to be too controversial, too risky, and too complex to be addressed with undergraduate students. Yet, they also believed, and it was borne out in the study, that without such dialogue, practicing teachers would only continue to feel powerless to effectively conduct their classrooms and make a difference in their interactions with students. Though skeptical at the outset, Marx and Pennington were willing to take the risk, and as a consequence of this study, they strongly encourage continued engagement with the topic in teacher preparation courses at both undergraduate and graduate levels.

Marx and Pennington's findings and recommendations are compatible with the perspective of this professional development series with the following exception. In this series *"Whiteness" is viewed more broadly and applicable to all who are steeped in dominant culture ideology.* Clearly, to operate classrooms according to the dominant prevailing culture only is to indoctrinate and encapsulate students in dominant-culture ideology.

Manifestations of the dominant mainstream culture in the nation's schools and the often tragic relationship of the dominant culture with the five cultures of color, has to be addressed if we are to make progress in building cross-cultural understanding and pursuing excellence in student learning. This, of course begins with knowing the *full history of American education* and its lasting impact in American schools. After reading and contemplating the broad historical panorama of American education, and then looking up close at the historical research on your own culture, you can begin to analyze commonly accepted practices in classrooms. In this sense, you are on the threshold of obtaining cultural competence. The next module continues to set the stage for culturally competent classroom practice as it orients you to a philosophy and way of thinking to guide your classroom practices. You should find the process to be significant as you continue to contemplate the kind of classroom you wish to have.

Related to the ideas presented in this module, the twelve culturally diverse classroom practitioners were asked to share their views. Their opinions and insights are provided below.

Classroom Teachers Talk It Over

"I have a basic understanding of the theories of education, Piaget, Vgotsky, and Montessori, but I never focused on the reasons behind the formation of schools and how that relates to what we do in schools today. Come to think of it, I did learn about Horace Mann but I remember very little about him."

"I always had a dislike for history. Now I know why. What I learned in my history classes just didn't seem relevant. Now I see that it can be interesting and informative."

"I never really knew about the history of these cultural groups, and I am really disappointed that we don't receive a full and accurate account of history in our high school and college courses."

"Learning about this history makes me very sad to know that our country caused problems for other cultures. I wish I could be more positive, but I am ashamed."

"Honestly I just never paid much attention to historical foundations of American schools even though I believe that it could help me understand schools today."

"No wonder African Americans wanted a Black History month. During this month was the only time I learned very much about African American history."

"I don't know much right now but I am eager to learn the history of different cultures because I believe that history shapes each person's existence and, knowing a person's culture can develop tolerance and empathy toward them."

"Knowledge of history can help me create awareness with students, and be a true facilitator to help students understand each other better. I believe that when I know the history of groups of people it is easier to understand their culture and use this knowledge as a source of background knowledge in my classroom interactions with them."

As you conclude this module, consider the views of these teachers and be prepared to give your view? How do your thoughts about cultural history compare with the views expressed by these classroom practitioners?

A Summary of Learning in Module Two

This module was designed to give you an introduction to the history of five representative cultural groups in relationship to the dominant American cultural group. Its major purpose has been to show you how this history has affected the way schools and classrooms operate today. In review, some specific points are:

- History tells you how things came to be as they are. Knowing the history of the common school helps you to understand the cultural perspective of schooling, and to see how today's public schools came to be as they are. Schooling for the five representative cultural groups, not included in the formation and development of the public school, was very different. This understanding is very significant as you seek to understand schools today.

- Cultural history insights can be gained through a study of your historical background and the terminology that has emanated from cultural history. You should understand and be able to explain your cultural history and background in relationship to the cultural groups studied in this module.

- Now that you have a general overview of the history of Anglo-American culture and its dominance in American schools and society, you should have a better understanding of why and how this culture predominates in American schools.

- The brief histories of the five major cultural groups—Latin American, Native American, African American, Asian American, and Arab/Muslim American—in today's schools in relationship to the dominant American culture can help you see the hardships they faced en route to America and the necessity of undertaking the recommended classroom practices of this professional development series.

- You have been able to see that there are dominant/non-dominant culture issues which continue to restrict cross-cultural understanding in today's schools. You should have learned the intricate language as it has evolved in the country's lexicon as a result of tension in the interactions between dominant and non-dominant cultural groups. Clearly, use of the terms and concepts presented in the module continues to cause tension as the country attempts to move beyond this history.

Cultural enlightenment is clearly dependent upon your knowledge of history from the early formation of schools to today. This module has concentrated on giving you basic information about the role that history has played in influencing the perceptions and interactions of cultural groups in America. The residue of much of this history persists in today's classrooms. In the next module, you gain a perspective on ways that you can analyze and begin to make the changes that cultural competence requires.

Opening Scenario (Afterthoughts)

How would you describe the dilemma faced by the history teacher at the beginning of the module after studying the material in Module Two? Please give examples to explain some specific insights that you have gained from the module.

The following questions, exercises, and activities will help you assess your level of cultural competence upon completion of Module Two.

Questions/Activities

1. Explain how the study of your cultural history has influenced your thinking.

2. Compare and contrast the educational history and the schooling of each cultural group with the dominant mainstream culture. What are some implications of this history for classroom teachers?

3. Explain the following concepts in relationship to the history of the <u>dominant mainstream culture</u> in America:

    Manifest Destiny   ethnocentrism   cultural imperialism
    Deculturation   melting pot   cultural assimilation

4. Explain the following concepts in relationship to the history of <u>non-dominant cultures</u> in America:

   minority group   prejudice   cultural inversion   ethnic   racism

<u>Cooperative Group Activity:</u>

Read further to obtain additional information on the history of the five cultural groups presented in this chapter. Present your findings to the class in a panel discussion.

Looking in Classrooms

Visit classrooms in your area to observe the extent to which history is conveyed in the classroom environment. Observe and note the following. (Ask questions in areas where you need clarification):

1. In what ways is the dominant culture depicted in the classroom? And to what extent is the teacher aware of this phenomenon?

2. In what ways are other cultural groups displayed in the classroom? To what extent is the teacher aware of this?

Then, write a brief <u>Descriptive Summary Statement</u> to explain what depictions of history are displayed in the classroom and any other practices related to history that you observed in this setting. What would you do in your own classroom to enhance cultural understanding through the study of history?

Recommendations for Further Reading

Cremin, Lawrence. *The American Common School: An Historic Conception.* New York: Teachers College Press, 1951.

    From this source, readers can obtain a comprehensive historical account of the formation of what has become the American public school.

Spring, Joel. *The American School 1642-2004.* New York: McGraw-Hill, 2005.

    Spring highlights the histories of multiple cultural groups in relation to dominant American cultural groups.

Takaki, Ronald. *A Different Mirror: A History of Multicultural America.* Boston: Little Brown and Company, 1993.

    In this book, readers obtain an alternative account of the histories of multiple cultures in America.

Zinn, Howard. *A Peoples History of the United States 1492-Present.* New York: Harper Collins, 1999.

    Zinn writes about American history from the perspectives of the people who lived it rather than from the government. The perspective he presents is very revealing.

Module Three

Critical Pedagogy as a Process to Facilitate Cross-Cultural Understanding and Excellence in Learning

Opening Scenario...76

Key Concepts...79

Topics Covered in this Module:

- How Critical Pedagogy Facilitates a Culturally-Inclusive Classroom Philosophy...79

- The Language of Critical Pedagogy...83

- Using Critical Pedagogy to Analyze Current Classroom Practices...87

    Eurocentric Practices...88

    Religious and Patriotic Holidays...88

    Curriculum and Teaching Practices...90

- Promoting Access to the "Culture of Power:" A Step toward Cross-Cultural Understanding and Excellence in Learning...92

- Multiple Perspectives as Enabling to Cross-Cultural Understanding and Excellence in Learning...95

    Multiple Perspectives as a Goal...95

    Overcoming the Impediments...97

Classroom Teachers Talk It Over...98

Summary of Learning in Module Three…99

Opening Scenario (Afterthoughts)…101

Questions/Activities…101

Looking in Classrooms…102

Recommendations for Further Readings…103

Opening Scenario

While visiting an elementary school during the week just before Thanksgiving the university supervisor in charge of student teachers at the school notes that the regular academic program in the kindergarten and first grade classes have been suspended to make preparations for the school's traditional Thanksgiving celebrations. The young students have made tepees, colorful headdresses with feathers, and other attire to represent the American view of the Indians who celebrated the first Thanksgiving with the Pilgrims. The students have also made Pilgrim hats and other black and white costumes to depict the Pilgrims at this celebration. These activities have taken much of the month of November as all of the kindergarten and first grade classes have made preparations for this holiday.

The students are very excited as they take on their roles as either Pilgrims or Indians, put on their costumes, and get ready for the program. As the program begins, those portraying Indians put on their feathers and make the sounds that have come to be identified with Indians. The pilgrims stand erect and welcome the Indians to the feast. The feast includes vegetable soup, popcorn, and candy. The teachers very enthusiastically explain that this is a traditional holiday that is celebrated in this manner every year. The students are very excited about it, the teachers see it as a routine part of the kindergarten program, the parents expect it, and the school administration supports it. The student interns simply view it as the way things are done in schools without giving much thought to it at all. More than likely, it is the way it was done when they were in elementary school, and very likely they will operate their classrooms similarly.

What are your thoughts about this holiday celebration and the way in which it is carried out in the classroom? How would you describe the cultural frame of reference of the teachers in these classrooms? How are they alike or unlike you as you begin this module of the professional development series? As you reflect on the history of Native Americans from your study in Module Two, what perceptions do you have as you begin this module?

As you prepare to become or continue your role as a teacher in today's world of culturally diverse classrooms, you can probably identify with situations where these traditional holidays are celebrated in American schools, especially in elementary grade classrooms. What challenges do these traditions pose for you as you seek to develop cross-cultural understanding in your classroom?

This module discusses the third of the cultural competencies that Volume I under takes to prepare you to conduct your classroom to build cross-cultural understanding and promote excellence in student learning. It provides a process for examining current practices in classrooms, as an important step in designing effective culturally-inclusive classroom practices. This module builds on the first two modules of this volume. It continues the goal of developing your cultural competence by challenging you to take your cultural and historical knowledge about America's schools and relate it to current practices in today's classrooms. You are asked to adopt a critical eye toward things as they are. This analysis makes it possible for you to contemplate the changes that you would make in your classroom, and begin to formulate your classroom philosophy. Through critical pedagogy you come to see that many classroom practices, which may have seemed innocuous at first glance, upon closer examination, operate to inhibit cross-cultural understanding and thwart excellence in learning. Then, by understanding and coming to terms with the "culture of power" and its use as a source of empowerment for you and your students, you can begin to plan for your very complex role in today's classrooms.

Let me state up front that you may find this module to be the most provocative of the series. Surely, you have already found areas of Volume I to be thought provoking as compared with other books on education topics. This module moves even further beyond the realm of what you have been used to reading and hearing from educators. When I used some of this material with undergraduate and graduate students, many found it intriguing, particularly the new information and way of thinking, and the constructed language to explain the concepts. Others said they benefited significantly from the reading but felt threatened along the way. It was the idea of relearning and unlearning what they thought they knew about schooling and the acceptance of critique regarding educational practice without taking it personally that frustrated most. I considered these reactions in my writing of this module, but then I also thought, "My goal is to have you become what Giroux refers to in this module as a transforming intellectual. I want you to think before acting rather than to merely accept and act without thinking." It is therefore important, I believe, that you actively engage with the provocative material in this module. My suggestion is simply to read it with an open mind. If you do, I promise that you will learn and grow from the experience.

The module begins with critique and ends with possibility. Through the process, it proposes principles and practices that can contribute to your competence in the classroom. Upon completion of this module, you should be more attuned to the intricacies of classroom practice and you should have a more coherent world view and philosophical orientation. At this point you will be on the threshold of having the cultural competence necessary to develop classroom policies and practices which can lead your students to cross-cultural understanding and excellence in learning.

As you study this module, you should focus on answering the following key questions:

- How will a critical pedagogy perspective enhance your cultural competence and classroom management skill?

- What do you learn about the unique language of critical pedagogy and how does it help to build your cultural competence?

- How can you use critical pedagogy to help you analyze traditional classroom practices, why they inhibit cross cultural understanding, and what does this awareness have for you in your role as a classroom teacher?

- What is the "culture of power" and how can you use it as a source of empowerment in teaching and working with culturally diverse students?

- How can empathy and multiple perspectives lessen the impediments to cross-cultural understanding that exist in many American classrooms?

Key Concepts

critical pedagogy ~ conscientization ~ discourse ~ compulsory education law ~ problem posing ~ dialectic ~ transformative knowledge ~ dialogue ~ sanitizing ~ emancipatory knowledge ~ literacy ~ ethnocentric curriculum ~ cultural capital ~ hidden curriculum ~ culture of power ~ grooming ~ voice ~ sustaining ambivalence ~ ideology ~ Eurocentric ~ bicultural ~ hegemony ~ egocentrism principle ~ double consciousness ~ tracking ~ perspective taking ~ schemata ~ indirect teaching ~ direct instruction

How Critical Pedagogy Facilitates a Culturally-Inclusive Classroom Philosophy

Cultural competence calls for having information and the inclination to act on that information. **Critical pedagogy** is an all-encompassing philosophical orientation to guide you in analyzing classrooms and in designing and conducting your own classroom. Critical pedagogy enables you to display your cultural competence, formulate a culturally-inclusive mindset, and act on what you know to be true. It sets up the conditions for you to confront, challenge and, where necessary, make changes in the way your classroom operates. It calls for unlearning much of what you thought you knew in favor of an inclusive classroom philosophy.

The theory, introduced in the pivotal book, Teachers as Intellectuals (Giroux, 1988), and carried forth in the more recent book, Life in Schools (McLaren, 2007), parallels the series' philosophical perspective. Joan Wink (Wink, 2005), who explains the practical applications of critical pedagogy, introduces a special language to convey the philosophy. Theirs is a philosophy and language of critique and of possibility. Their language of critique asks us to take off our blinders and begin to see clearly. Their language of possibility leads us to perspective taking, to approach other persons or cultures on their terms rather than on preconceived terms of what we would like the other to be. The provocative nature of their writings and their colorful terminology is designed to challenge and ultimately take you to places you know but have been afraid to acknowledge. From their writings, you can gain insight into the intricate ways that the dominant culture retains power and control, including subtleties you very likely have never thought about.

Giroux's success at confronting the structured silence of history as it exists in American schools, and at offering a new vision grounded in hope and liberating struggle, has made him a significant educational theorist. He is concerned that you and other teachers act as intellectuals. As a result, he accentuates pedagogical empowerment through the curriculum, teaching, and classroom practices within schools. He argues that both you and your students must be educated to intervene in the struggle to restructure the conditions of the wider society. This, he believes, calls for you and your colleagues to be *transforming intellectuals.* Giroux's primary interest has been to empower those for whom history has dealt a cruel blow and foreclosed a future of hope. He includes among this group the indigent and disaffected, but also, *those of more privileged positions who have been either too intransigent or powerless to take a stand against the inequities and injustices of society.*

Giroux challenges the traditional use of classroom practice as an avenue for passing on a "common culture" and set of skills to serve the present social order. Instead, he is concerned with helping students, particularly those from the oppressed class, recognize that the dominant culture is not neutral nor is it well-intentioned by revealing its myths and injustices (Giroux 1988, 7). Giroux believes that your teaching must go beyond simply making knowledge and experiences relevant to your students. He believes you must also challenge yourself and your students to *look for the hidden assumptions which support this knowledge and experience,* and then transform that knowledge by having the courage to intervene. He explains the power/knowledge construct that is instrumental in the role that you and your colleagues should play as critically engaged intellectuals in this manner:

> Knowledge can no longer be seen as objective, but has to be understood as part of the power relations that not only produce it but also those who benefit from it. Every form of knowledge can be located within

specific power relations; as time passes certain forms of knowledge are transformed by ruling groups into "regimes of truth"…an essential step in helping teachers challenge existing "regimes of truth" can best be achieved if teachers assume the role of transformative intellectuals… committed to… teaching as an emancipatory practice…. (Giroux 1988, xviii)

Peter McLaren, another cultural theorist and colleague of Giroux, builds on the perspective set forth in Giroux's 1988 book. McLaren begins with the premise that men and women are essentially "un-free" and inhabit a world rife with contradictions and asymmetric power and privilege" (McLaren 2007, p.194). He believes that teachers in general, have been conditioned to accept the familiar as inevitable, and without intervention, he says you are likely to follow this same line of reasoning. He asks you, instead, to think beyond the inevitability of present and recurring circumstances in classrooms, to see schooling as essentially partisan, and to think of classrooms as sites that can promote both domination and liberation. Like Giroux, McLaren believes that those of you who are *classroom teachers need to look critically so you can see that what you do in your classrooms is not a neutral act for, if you see yourself as neutral, you are on the side of the dominant culture.* Every time you choose a curriculum or method of teaching, you are making a political choice "What will I teach and what won't I teach, how, why, and to whom will I teach or not teach?" Even though the knowledge base and instructional process may be research based, they are also political. Both are political choices; to teach is to take a stand. You need to see that there are more than two equal sides to an issue; there are many sides which need to be examined in light of societal forces and then weighed and balanced toward emancipatory interests.

McLaren sees empowerment as coming from knowledge and social relations that dignify one's history, language, and cultural traditions. He believes that you need to know and actively teach the cultural and historical context surrounding the endeavors in your classroom. How you, your students, and others define what you do according to the dominant culture paradigm is of central pedagogical concern because it helps you to understand how classroom meaning is produced and made legitimate or illegitimate (McLaren 2007, 214).

A belief system which is built on understanding yourself while also understanding the dominant culture and your relationship to it, can cause you to move beyond a comfortable but limiting lifestyle, to a more inclusive and embracing way of teaching, living, and being. When you are a teacher, who embraces a critical pedagogy orientation, you have a vision regarding your presence in the world and your role in teaching. You are passionate about making a difference and are in the continuous state of becoming. You have the humility to recognize that through teaching, you also learn. You choose not to "go with the flow" or be complacent about and accepting of the status quo or bureaucratization of mind that takes place in many day-to-day classrooms. Instead, you *continually question the very nature of education and the role of schools. You dream dreams about changing reality through the schools and about making the world a better place.* Critical pedagogy is the glue, the theoretical perspective that makes it all fit. Therefore, it is presented as a process in this module to enable you to see beyond where you are in your current thinking, and begin to see new possibilities for your classroom.

Joan Wink (2005), a critical pedagogy practitioner, gives an intriguing, introspective, and practical presentation of the work of Giroux, McLaren, and other critical pedagogy theorists in her book, Critical Pedagogy: Notes from the Real World. Her account is particularly useful because it offers interesting, colorful, descriptive definitions and explanations for the complex and evolving concepts associated with critical pedagogy. She begins by analyzing the concept of critical pedagogy itself with the caution that, even though there is a critical dimension to critical pedagogy, it does not simply mean to criticize. Critical, in her view, calls for thinking about and analyzing what is *below the surface*. She sees pedagogy as more than the way a teacher teaches. Pedagogy, in the context of critical pedagogy, is at the heart of effective classroom practice. *It concerns the human interactions, both visible and hidden, between teachers and students in classrooms and how this socialization transfers to the larger community.* Critical pedagogy, then, can be thought of as a prism that reflects the complexities of classroom interactions by highlighting some of the hidden subtleties that are easily overlooked. Joan Wink makes the point that, after looking through the prism of critical pedagogy, the basics may not be as basic as once believed (Wink, 2005).

Joan Wink sets the stage for you to have a critical, yet facilitating mind set; that is, to have the knowledge base and the inclination to *change* what is. She sees a critical pedagogy thought process as developing in a learning-relearning-unlearning cycle. For example, you begin the process by *learning,* through your upbringing and schooling to understand and behave in certain ways according to the dictates of the culture. Then, as you obtain new information and insights from this material, additional study, and your experiences in classrooms, you are *relearning* by adding information and insights that come from experience of what goes on in the real-world of schools and classrooms to your store of knowledge. After noting inconsistencies between what you had learned previously and what you are currently learning and experiencing, you are ready to move to the next step which is *unlearning.* Unlearning is the most difficult because it involves a shift in philosophy or beliefs to let go of the knowledge you once thought you had. It is hard to let go of knowledge that is comfortably entrenched in one's schema, but unlearning is central to critical pedagogy. Once you obtain new information to challenge previously held beliefs, there is often a spin-off and other things previously taken for granted are also subject to challenge. Unlearning is the paradigm shift from the passive to active learning that is the essence of cultural competence.

To fully grasp the power of critical pedagogy, you can enter into the dynamics and language of this new perspective which such writers as Giroux, McLaren, Wink, and others have introduced into the field of education. The body of knowledge and associated terms and concepts that are developing around the relationship between dominant and non-dominant groups, exposes and puts a name to the circumstances that non-dominant groups have experienced in relationship to the dominant culture paradigm. The concepts and terminology will have even greater meaning when considered in the context of your cultural and historical understandings as discussed in the previous two modules. In your quest for cultural competence, familiarity with this new perspective and the language associated with it can help you analyze and explain the activities of present-day schools and classrooms. Do they inhibit or facilitate cross-cultural understanding and learning excellence? Armed with a critical pedagogy perspective and language, you can begin to consider and articulate your own view of classroom practice.

The Language of Critical Pedagogy

The construct, *Conscientization*, is the first of the concepts that can help us gain insights into our power to change things as they are. Conscientization has to do with coming to understand based on our knowledge and experiences, and having confidence in that knowledge. *It is the power that we have when we know that we know and have the courage to challenge and find ways to alter practices that are inconsistent with that knowledge.* Knowing what questions to ask and what to look for gets the ball rolling.

Problem posing opens the door to asking questions and seeking answers to questions that many do not want to hear. It brings critical inquiry and interactive participation into the existing state of affairs. Whereas problem solving brings about a feel-good sensation, problem posing may engender uncomfortable feelings, for problem posing is often concerned with challenging existing norms and conventions. New knowledge and insights are the vehicles for moving from problem posing to conscientization. *Transformative knowledge* promotes change in the composition and structure of our knowledge. And, through varying degrees of relearning and unlearning, it can become *emancipatory knowledge.* At the point of emancipation, knowledge becomes free from the restraint, control, and power of the dominant culture. We can have this level of knowledge when we *know that we know* and it is the basis for conscientization.

Cultural capital and grooming are methods that schools use to help non-dominant culture students attain mainstream status. These concepts are relevant to the later discussion on the "culture of power." **Cultural Capital** is mainstream western culture broken down into its component parts. It includes practices that are unconsciously determined by the dominant culture such as ways of moving, thinking, and talking that are used to determine success in American society. Schools generally value and reward those who exhibit dominant culture capital. The cultural capital traits exhibited by students such as politeness, industriousness, or students' manner of dressing and speaking tend to be looked upon by teachers as natural qualities. They are generally cultural in nature, however, and often linked to social class. Students from dominant culture homes inherit this cultural capital as opposed to their non-dominant culture peers having to ferret it out. ***Grooming*** is about preparing groups for mainstream status; it is the process for gaining cultural capital and access to the "culture of power." Upward mobility and movement into mainstream culture occurs through schooling and other sources of grooming. Success is bestowed upon those who are either in the dominant culture already, or who follow the path outlined by the dominant culture for admittance. One group, by virtue of its hereditary position in the dominant culture, has the advantage while the other group in the process of ferreting it out, is often faced with a rough and rocky road filled with obstacles along the way. Race, class, and gender continue to be variables that determine which group gets the breaks and which group gets the hurdles.

Ideology and hegemony can help us gain a deeper understanding of how the dominant culture has been put into place. ***Ideology*** is a systematic body of content or thinking characteristic of an individual, group, or culture, and maintained through its customs, beliefs, and rituals. Cultures organize reality according to their ideology. Dominant culture ideologies are given prominence in American society and are presented, and sustained through the media, the schools, other institutions, and the family. The dominant culture exercises domination over subordinate groups through a process called ***hegemony***, the domination of one group over another. The dominant group determines and controls knowledge and literacy. It is a struggle in which those who are oppressed are led by those in power through schools and other societal institutions to participate in their own oppression. If we do not conduct our classrooms in ways that encourage students to question the prevailing values, attitudes, and practices of the dominant culture in a systematic and critical way, our classrooms will, in effect, preserve the hegemony of the dominant culture.

Language and its use are the means for giving form to a more critical self en route to emancipation from the grips of the dominant culture power structure. Discourse, dialectic, and dialogue form the language dimensions in critical pedagogy. **Discourse** is an expression of thought on a subject. In discourse words carry messages about power, what knowledge is appropriate or inappropriate, which voices are heard and which are marginalized, what knowledge is valued and what knowledge is devalued. Discourse is socially and culturally grounded and involves the use of loaded words such as "at-risk," "limited English proficient," "normal," "mainstream," etc. In classrooms, dominant culture discourse determines what books to use, what approaches to employ, and what values and beliefs to transmit. **Dialectic** refers to the tension between opposing thoughts, ideas, values, and beliefs, seeing and articulating contradictions or views in opposition to one's own. Dialectic is the process of learning from the opposing view to obtain a more comprehensive understanding of an issue. Dialectic, as a methodology, attempts to tease out the histories and relations, the bigger picture, of accepted meaning from context to part, or system to event. A version of this methodology is applied in Volume IV as an aspect of culturally transformative teaching. Classrooms which incorporate dialectic are seen as cultural arenas of empowerment and transformation. **Dialogue**, in the sense of "talking back" is language that can lead to meaningful change. It is profound, wise, insightful conversation that creates and recreates multiple understandings. It changes people or their context, moving them to the uncomfortable place of relearning and unlearning. Genuine thoughtful dialogue, used skillfully as an instructional approach, enables students to see subtle ethnocentric bias. The opportunity for us as classroom teachers to set up our classrooms to encourage students to engage in such dialogue is addressed in the educational program described in Volume III. Our ability as classroom teachers to structure conditions so that the dispossessed will have voice is a major goal of critical pedagogy.

Voice is the use of language to describe the *substance* of one's reality, one's experience, one's world. In this society, the determination of whose voice or perspective gets to be expressed is determined by the dominant culture. Closely related to voice is the *process* used to silence perspectives or voices that run counter to the dominant power structure. Silencing has to do with the insidious way in which the agenda is set up to determine who speaks, who listens, and who gets heard. The lives of the many have been silenced and under the control of the powerful dominant culture, its perspective, viewpoint, and way of knowing. However, today with non-dominant cultures beginning to stake their claim in this society, the dominant culture is being forced to speak louder than ever to be heard.

Literacy is generally believed to be the primary aim of schools and classrooms; however, literacy and the ways in which it manifests itself in dominant culture schools deserve investigation. ***Literacy,*** defined as the underlying way of knowing, thinking and making complex meanings, is given priority in schools through its curriculum, books, and other means of gaining knowledge, as the avenue for transmitting the dominant culture to the next generation. The attempt to transmit this culture is not limited to just one subject; it is comprehensive and pervasive, touching all aspects of the educational enterprise. Literacy, in this sense, threatens the identity of other cultures by imposing the dominant culture's way of knowing on everyone. Illiteracy, as one of the loaded, value-laden concepts that is used to deny access to power, is the unfortunate derivative of literacy. Also, oracy, the oral element of literacy, is devalued by mainstream American culture. Orate people in this society may be equated to being illiterate. In many communities throughout the world, however, people are given high recognition for their ability to carry their knowledge in their heads and to convey it orally instead of on paper. Critical pedagogy calls for us to look at literacy as more than reading and writing. Literacy, considered more broadly, calls for *reading the world* and examining its surrounding power structures.

In schools, an examination of the power structure of the dominant culture calls for understanding the hidden curriculum. ***Hidden curriculum*** refers to the unintended practices, interactions and outcomes of the schooling process. It deals with the tacit ways in which knowledge and behavior are constructed outside of the formally scheduled educational program. The unexpressed perpetuation of the dominant culture through the institutional processes and practices of the hidden curriculum is at the heart of classroom practice. This includes the unspoken rules of conduct, classroom organization, recognitions and celebrations, pedagogical procedures, governance structures, and teacher expectations. Much of what students learn—norms, values, and beliefs—emanate from the hidden curriculum. It takes a critical lens to bring the hidden qualities of this informal curriculum to the surface. Critical pedagogy theorist, Henry Giroux, calls for making the hidden curriculum explicit, a task that is undertaken in this professional development series by emphasizing and explaining how to teach explicitly the often tacitly generated classroom practice structures, procedures, and expectations.

Critical pedagogy asks those of us, who are teachers in the classrooms of this country, to come to the point of conscientization, and this means understanding these critical pedagogy concepts. To understand the concepts, though, is to know more than their meanings. We can begin to see the impact and means used by the dominant culture to convey its ideology and hegemony through the language of discourse, and we can learn how to alter it through the language of dialectic and dialog. When we know that we know and have the courage to act on that knowledge, we will find ways to incorporate its features in our classroom practices.

As Joan Wink advises, critical pedagogy teaches teachers to name, but also to reflect critically, and then to act. This suggests that the substance reflected in the language of critical pedagogy needs to be integrated into classroom policies and procedures to become the means of classroom practice. We are therefore advised to come to terms with this way of viewing our role in the classroom by relearning, and unlearning much of what we had previously learned in light of our evolving knowledge and experiences. With critical pedagogy, we have a new consciousness and process for observing and thinking about classroom practices as they occur. Understanding the intricacies of the language that has come to be associated with critical pedagogy gives us labels for what we are learning intellectually, to be able to speak critically without showing scorn for those who are caught in the grip of dominant culture intransigence or lack of knowledge.

You can use critical pedagogy as a framework to develop a philosophy, which defines your classroom as a source of possibility wherein you can enable all students to operate from a position of empowerment. The process of defining and implementing such a philosophy won't be immediate or easy; it will be incremental with advances and setbacks. In the process, as a more empowered classroom teacher, you will be able to use the struggles that occur within day-to-day classroom events and activities as opportunities for transformative and emancipatory growth. What happens within your classroom can then go out into the community to make life better.

Using Critical Pedagogy to Analyze Classroom Practices

Taking all that you are learning about critical pedagogy as a philosophical framework, we can now engage in the learning-relearning-unlearning cycle of critical pedagogy as we examine classroom practices we all took for granted during our upbringing and K-12 schooling. Classroom practice includes a range of events and activities and a myriad of decisions that are under our control. While we, as classroom teachers, may not take full advantage of our opportunities, we have considerable discretion in determining many classroom practices. For example, The process of teaching, student interaction patterns, the way that the rules and procedures for classroom operation are established and enforced, how consequences for student misbehavior are enacted, and the methods used for resolving conflict are all within your decision making domain. This section will help you examine what goes on in classrooms and consider the implications of some classroom practices that you might not have noticed before.

As part of the cycle of learning-relearning-unlearning, it is worthwhile for you to reflect on what you have learned about the relationship between culture and classroom practice in Module One and the history of schooling in Module Two. Then together, we can tour some classrooms like those in which I have been intimately involved over several decades, and take a critical look at what is still taking place inside. I will provide commentary about the practices and issues involved as we go. Our primary focus will be on three categories of day-to-day practice: Eurocentric practices, practices centered on religious and patriotic holidays, and the types of teacher-student interactions that are prevalent in these classrooms.

Eurocentric Practices

First, let us look inside a variety of classrooms and apply critical pedagogy to analyze some of the day-to-day practices. You recall from Module Two that these overarching *Eurocentric* principles and practices of the public schools have their roots in the history of the American common school. Now, as you look around, you can see that the Anglo-European based classroom practices are ubiquitous, coloring everything that occurs from the bulletin boards to the songs that are sung, and the games that are played. Students, subtly and sometimes not so subtly, are influenced to accept the Eurocentric American way as "The Way." The omnipresence of this American way and its institutional arrangements are taken for granted. As a result, it is not necessary to use overt means to maintain a position of advantage. The invisible hand is always there, compelling everyone to act routinely in concert with its cultural assumptions and interests.

There is also the well-established *egocentrism principle* "me-first, then family, community, state, then nation" ideology which governs the elementary school social studies curriculum combined with the principles of "winning at all costs," and "every one for himself or herself." These principles are rooted in Anglo-American culture and, as we have seen from the brief historical accounts of the cultural groups that make up American schools, many of these practices are hard to embrace by many of the world's cultures.

Religious and Patriotic Holiday Practices

Let us now continue the tour by looking more closely at another of the common classroom practices which may seem innocuous on its face. The well-established monolithic way in which religious and patriotic holidays are handled in schools and classrooms is worthy of note. As we look into the prevalence of these religious and patriotic holiday practices, it is helpful to recall that the early founders wanted an educational system centered on Anglo-Saxon values, religion, and patriotism and they used this hegemony to subjugate and colonize nations such as Puerto Rico.

It is also important for you to understand the ways in which current law and this desire of the founders intertwine and diverge. The most basic thing to understand is that the **compulsory education law** requires equal access. Because students are compelled into classrooms on a random basis with little in common with their classmates and teacher, the standard of insuring equal access is higher than it would be in other public institutions without such compulsion. Students who attend public schools bring with them their cultural and family values which may range from being fundamentalist Christian to being Atheist to being Buddhist to being Hindu.

The celebration of holidays and other customs, to which some families are wedded while others may find objectionable, is an area in need of examination by school officials rather than outright acceptance on the premise of clinging to tradition. A few examples can help to illustrate why we should be concerned. Many school and classroom activities are scheduled around and centered on religious or patriotic holidays such as Christmas, Thanksgiving, Easter, Halloween, and Columbus Day, which reflect the values of the dominant culture while many non-dominant cultures have no ties to these customs. Consider such activities, often seen at the elementary more than secondary level, as the Thanksgiving Day celebration between the Pilgrims and Indians described in the introductory scenario, or the commemoration of Columbus Day. And try to imagine the feelings of horror and dread that the Native American community must experience each year when faced with reliving the school's tradition of reenacting these two events. Then there are the children of Jehovah's Witnesses, whose families celebrate no holidays. The list goes on…

In actuality, if the dominant culture were not so pervasive and entrenched in the schools, teachers themselves might be more likely to give greater scrutiny, and take action to curtail such practices. Celebrating such holidays, they recognize, has minimal relationship to the already overcrowded prescribed curriculum. Clearly, there are fundamental reasons to take a critical look at these holidays and customs. To overlook culturally-insensitive practices such as these that are being imparted in many classrooms would be contrary to the spirit of sustaining positive family-school relationships and to building cross-cultural understanding.

Since you are now a more attuned and sensitive classroom teacher, your knowledge, your influence, and *your actions,* can serve as the catalyst for change in these classroom practices. The goal would not be to appease everyone by simply to adding on more holidays, one for each represented cultural group, but through conscientization to come to terms with the ramifications of these ongoing traditions and their effect on cultural relations. Excellence in student learning demands this attention.

Curriculum and Teaching Practices

A third area to analyze in our tour and examination of a variety of classroom practices that should be of great significance to us as educators is what and how teachers teach. Some practices to be noted include the teaching methods that are employed, the ways that teachers handle non-dominant culture material, grouping arrangements to handle diversity in student learning, and teacher style and interaction patterns. Then through the lens of critical pedagogy we can summarize our findings and their meaning for cross-cultural understanding and excellence in student learning.

From this tour of a variety of classrooms it becomes clear that the teaching methods which most teachers use de-contextualize learning for non-dominant culture students. When this happens, there is incongruity between theory and practice. Overwhelming research and agreement among cognitive psychologists and theorists confirm that meaningful learning is dependent upon integrating new material with student's existing *schemata*, that prior experiences provide the foundation for interpreting new information. Yet, when the prior experiences of those who differ from mainstream norms are disregarded, learning for these students is fragmented and without foundation.

It is also clear from our tour and observations of a variety of teacher-student interchanges that many teachers in their day-to-day teaching are reluctant to expose students to view-points which may be in conflict with mainstream thinking, or to engage students in discussion about any other perspective. Of course, this is understandable since many teachers have limited background knowledge with material other than the dominant-culture. And, given these circumstances, we can agree that such discussions are better left alone because they could be demoralizing to all concerned. But, if teachers don't have the knowledge and background to teach from other cultural perspectives, or to bring topics that may be considered controversial to light, the cultural frame of reference of students and institutional policies will remain unchanged, students will continue to be disempowered, and excellence in learning will continue to suffer.

Related to teacher's reluctance to engage meaningfully with controversial material, is the tendency of those who write textbooks, and for teachers themselves, to engage in *sanitizing*, to make the lives and accomplishments of bold revolutionary men and women acceptable for school use. Sonia Nieto explains how this works:

> The process of "sanitizing" is nowhere more evident than in a current depiction of Martin Luther King, Jr. In attempting to make him palatable to the mainstream, schools have made Martin Luther

King a Milquetoast. The only thing most children know about him is that he kept having a dream. Bulletin boards are full of ethereal pictures of Dr. King surrounded by clouds. If children get to hear any of his speeches at all, it is his "I Have a Dream" speech. As inspirational as this speech is, it is only one of his notable accomplishments. Martin Luther King, a man full of passion and life, becomes lifeless. He becomes a safe hero. (Nieto 2000, 348)

The curriculum and its delivery are areas of crucial significance for both cross-cultural understanding and learning excellence. In our tour of a variety of classrooms and looking closely at what and how teachers teach, it seems certain that any possibility for cross-cultural understanding and excellence in student learning are substantially foreclosed. What it takes to be considered literate in American schools is but a fraction of the available knowledge and those who make the choices about what is to be included in the curriculum seem influenced by their limited background and experiences. Because so many view-points are left out, mainstream and non-mainstream students alike receive, at best, a partial education. Being schooled in such a system encourages young people to develop an unrealistic view of the world and their place in it. In such an *ethnocentric curriculum* cross-cultural understanding is severely constrained. Students from non-dominant cultures are prone to develop feelings of inferiority and, because their culture tends to be glorified in such an ethnocentric presentation, students from the dominant culture tend to develop feelings of superiority. Both feelings are based on limited, inaccurate information about the world, and both are harmful.

Also worthy of comment, though hard to discern in a limited tour is the tentative manner in which many teachers present information and give directives to students—whether they use a direct or indirect approach. In *indirect teaching*, discussed in Volume IV as facilitative teaching, students are generally faced with tasks that require them to figure out things for themselves with minimal direction from the teacher. Often, these tasks and the process of figuring them out are unfamiliar to students, particularly to students from non-dominant culture backgrounds. Another example of the indirect/tentative style occurs when teachers give disciplinary commands through such approaches as, "Don't you think it would be a good idea if you…," or, "What do you think you should do…?" These indirect requests deserve reconsideration for all students but, in particular, they can be inhibiting to those not familiar with what goes on in U.S. classrooms, and are trying to learn the nuances of the dominant-culture's expectations.

Finally, in our tour of classrooms and their practices, you could see students grouped within classrooms and even across classrooms according to ability. This often occurs in the area of reading and math, but sometimes students are assigned by ability and placed in one class for all subjects. Upon closer scrutiny, you may have noticed that a number of these students are from non-dominant cultures who have been placed in these homogeneous groups according to dominant-culture criteria. The common practice of *tracking* begins in elementary grades and carries forth through high school where it is standard practice in schools across the nation.

Together we engaged in the critical pedagogy cycle of learning-relearning-unlearning as we toured a variety of classrooms and looked in depth at Eurocentric classroom practices, religious and patriotic holiday practices, and curriculum and teaching practices. Through critical pedagogy and based on new information from this volume we were able to analyze and relearn classroom practices we all took for granted as part of our upbringing and K-12 schooling. Through conscientization we can now begin to move beyond practices such as these that have become customary in American classrooms. Remember, though, that unlearning ways that are entrenched after decades of living with them in our schools and homes will not be easy. However, we can become transforming intellectuals and use our discretion and decision-making power to determine and put into practice approaches to expand the horizons of all of our students. This professional development series is designed to help you unlearn much of what seemed natural at the time by offering alternative practical culturally-compatible practices. In the remaining three volumes you receive comprehensive practical assistance and strategies for designing and implementing culturally-inclusive classroom management, a culturally-centered educational program, and culturally-transformative teaching as a means of helping you complete the learning-relearning-unlearning cycle. Before getting into the three practical volumes of the series, let's reflect on our tour of classrooms and consider two important prerequisites for creating culturally attuned classrooms.

Promoting Access to the "Culture of Power:" A Step toward Cross-Cultural Understanding and Excellence in Learning

One important prerequisite is to overcome the domination and oppression by the dominant-culture power structure in schools and society and this begins with addressing the *"culture of power,"* the curriculum and methods of operating in U.S. schools and society. Several sources in this volume have pointed out that the culture of power can be a significant source of change in the quality of schooling for non-dominant culture students. It requires grooming the students to learn the essential qualities of the dominant "culture of power" so that they have the cultural capital to survive in his society and ultimately to alter this power structure.

Teaching the "culture of power" is emphasized throughout this series. The position taken is that through our classroom practices, we can teach students essential learning skills and also broaden their cultural perspectives. Non-dominant culture students in United States schools need to have an opportunity to learn the codes, rules, and methods of the "culture of power." At the same time, students need to retain their own culture and identity, a phenomenon referred to by W.E.B. DuBois as ***double consciousness.***

In the book, The Souls of Black Folk, W.E.B. DuBois, expressed this duality of being an American v. being a Negro as an inner psychological "twoness" of the African American psyche accordingly:

> The history of the American Negro is the history of this strife…to merge his double self into a better and truer self. In this merging he wishes neither of the older selves to be lost. He would not Africanize America…He would not bleach his Negro soul in a flood of white Americanism, for he knows that Negro blood has a message for the world. (DuBois 1961, 17)

"Sustaining ambivalence"—a state of being coined by T. J. Jackson Lears (1981) is used here as a stage en route to becoming ***bicultural***. Sustaining ambivalence in this sense calls for learning the ways of the dominant culture as a means to an end, while retaining the inherent qualities of one's culture of origin, identity, and comfort. It also means learning as much as possible about other cultures as well. The aim beyond this state is to be emancipatory, free of the dominant culture hegemony. It is also to be multicultural in one's overall being; that is, to be comfortable in interactions with multiple cultures in multiple societies. Knowing the power structure in the United States, its components and methods, is an important step in the effort to build an understanding of cultural relationships in this society.

Lisa Delpit (1995) embraces critical pedagogy and states very eloquently what is being stressed in this professional development series when she outlines some ways to think about the U.S. power structure and the "culture of power. She emphasizes that power manifests itself in classrooms in multiple ways. It shows up through the power of the teacher over the students, the power of the curriculum and textbooks to determine what view of the world is to be conveyed, the power of officials to determine who's intelligent and who's not and, ultimately, to determine the kind of job and socioeconomic status a person has. She also elaborates on what the "culture of power" values by explaining that there are codes or rules involving such practices as how a person presents him or herself through manner of speech, way of dressing, and style of interacting. She states further that institutions such as schools and workplaces presume a person's acquisition of this cultural capital. That is, they assume that people should know and be able to project themselves according to the standard of the dominant culture in America. Those who are part of the dominant culture presumably already have the tools to be successful in typical dominant culture environments and interactions; whereas, those who are not of this culture do not.

Delpit points out that the rules of the culture are a reflection of those who have power, and that those who have power are reluctant to have these rules taught to others, when she comments:

> "White educators had the authority to establish what was to be considered 'truth' regardless of the opinions of the people of color…and act under the assumption that to make any rules or expectations explicit is to …limit the freedom and autonomy of those subjected to the explicitness." (Delpit 1995, 26)

She also expands on the previously discussed critical pedagogy principles when she relates that dominant culture groups share these codes or rules because as co-members of the culture, they transmit the information implicitly to its members. Moreover, this power variable is likely to be internalized by those who have power to such an extent that they are unaware that they have such power. Those without power, however, detect it readily. Thus, *teaching the rules* associated with the "culture of power" makes it easier for those without power to attain it and use it as cultural capital for traversing effectively in American society. Your role, then, is to conscientiously groom students to be competent in the society in which they will work and live by teaching explicitly the context, information, rules, and codes of the dominant culture rather than leaving students "out there" to pick them up on their own. A direct approach in which teachers are clear and explicit in their classroom instructions is more appropriate, fair, and effective. **Direct instruction** as outlined in Volume IV is the precise purposeful teaching that is the vehicle for teaching the "culture of power." The "culture of power" thesis of teaching the dominant culture explicitly and well informs much of the thinking behind the practices to promote excellence in teaching and learning that are offered in this series.

We can now reflect and put our tour of classrooms and the rationale for teaching the culture of power in context. When considering previous discussions in this volume, it is easy to see why you might be perplexed about a proposal for directly teaching "the dominant culture's way." In this case, it is helpful for you to think both immediate and long term. Students need to know that there is a dominant culture that controls what goes on in schools and society and they need to be able to operate in this culture, but they also need to retain their identity, *who they are at the core.* These short-term accomplishments make it possible to move beyond the dominant culture standard and embrace other cultures in pursuit of an alternate more embracing and international style. Students will then have in their repertoire the means to transform American culture so that it truly becomes culturally inclusive. By having access to a full range of perspectives for thinking and becoming, the student is in a position to be more discriminating, cosmopolitan, and able to traverse comfortably in this country and in societies throughout the world.

Multiple Perspectives as Enabling to Cultural Understanding and Excellence in Learning

Together, we have looked critically at classrooms and have taken the step of empowering students to transform current conditions by learning the "culture of power." What is most needed as we move forward with the second prerequisite is your facilitating frame of mind to enrich your classroom with the perspectives of multiple cultures. The educational world of this 21st century can be a stimulating place for students and teachers, and, facing the challenges discussed in this module can be daunting, for sure. As a teacher in the new millennium, you may not have classrooms filled with quiet acquiescent students, or students who look like you do, but in a world without borders, your classroom will be filled with the richness of diversity. Meeting the challenge rests with you.

Multiple Perspectives as a Goal

When trying to understand issues associated with cultural diversity, the necessary frame of mind to adopt is one of ***perspective taking***, viewing situations through the eyes of another. Both you and your students need to be able to see the complexity of the world and the many perspectives involved. You need to be able to see that there are many ways of understanding reality, not just one, or two or three, and certainly not just the standard safe way. Take the example of slavery in the United States. In contrast to the traditional way of presenting the issue as slave holders against slaves, there are other perspectives that can come into play. What about the perspectives of poor White farmers, Black and White abolitionists, Native Americans who stood on the side of freedom, or the few Native Americans who themselves were slave holders. When you are able to get your students to see all of these perspectives, they can come to think of themselves as part of this history in ways that are not guilt-provoking or degrading. This same line of reasoning can be followed with the myriad of events, issues, practices, and circumstances that you and your students face in the classroom on a daily basis.

Understanding another culture is more difficult than copying it, however. Students are encouraged to use the process of perspective taking to seek their own truth rather than to paraphrase the thoughts of others. The practice of viewing situations through the eyes of another does not mean substituting one perspective for another. It aims, rather, to have those engaged in situations consider multiple and even contradictory perspectives in order to understand reality more fully. This frame of mind means respecting viewpoints for which there is disagreement. When the subject matter is society itself with all of its fallacies, exposing society's contradictions can be a meaningful classroom exercise for it requires enabling students to move knowledge from its current stage to the transformative stage, and then to the emancipatory stage. For example, discussions about concerns of power, poverty, discrimination, and war and their relationship to social justice might be topics that become transformative through thinking and talking about them, and then emancipatory if they lead toward putting the views into action for social justice.

Obviously this process needs to be tailored to and developmentally appropriate for the students. The process of confronting societies' contradictions is appropriate for high school and middle school students. Similarly, elementary students, who tend to have a strong sense of justice and fairness would also benefit from such exposure. In fact, viewing situations from multiple perspectives can be enhancing to all grade levels. Even younger elementary children can learn to think in this manner rather than in the customary (me, my family, my community, my state, my country) paradigm, where young children spend much of their earliest years learning about themselves and their immediate environment. Given what we now know about schooling, the more thoughtful question is not when will our *students* be ready to view situations from multiple perspectives, but when will we as *educators* have the courage and insight to be ready to teach them from multiple perspectives?

If we are to help students develop the level of cross-cultural understanding, the relationship between dominant and non-dominant cultures, that is essential to excellence in learning, we must address our own fears and insecurities. Then we must act in accord with our knowledge and beliefs for the process concerns relationships and attitudes more than subject matter. The work involved in setting up a Black History Month or a Mexican festival is easier by far than coming to terms with, and altering the way the curriculum depicts these two cultures or the way patriotic holidays influence the classroom practices of the elementary grades. These are just some of the parallels to illustrate what is needed.

To have impact on the way students interact and move toward cross-cultural understanding and excellence in learning, calls for *unlearning* conventional wisdom and dismantling policies that favor one group of students over another.

If you thought that you were being unbiased rather than partisan in your perspective on classroom practices, very likely you have now come to conscientization, to see that no part of the educational process is free from dominant culture influence. Critical pedagogy theorists have made it clear that to be neutral is to be on the side of the dominant culture. Therefore, to develop cross-cultural understanding the equation needs to be balanced in favor of other cultures. The issue, however, is not so much about whether students should learn the dominant culture nor is it about learning other cultures. Developing cross-cultural understanding as the foundation for excellence in learning involves helping students take on the perspectives of others, a facilitating quality for functioning effectively in multiple cultural and intellectual environments.

Overcoming the Impediments

As American educators, if we could come to the realization that learning excellence requires a mindset that says cultures throughout the world are important to know about and care about, cultural domination both here and abroad would lessen. As you recall from the historical account in Module Two, the schools and classrooms of America have been set up as the agencies responsible for enculturation and acculturation of students to the current dominant culture standard. Therefore, it does seems likely that the schools and classrooms of America can also be the agencies for helping students learn about and appreciate the ways of living of peoples throughout the world from *their* frame of reference as a more encompassing standard of excellence for school and classroom practice.

Achieving this standard could be filled with some frustration, however. Concentration on Western culture to the exclusion of learning about world cultures has caused U.S. students, as a rule, to be uninformed about the world and of other ways of seeing, thinking, and doing. *The towering presence and status of the United States in the world has created a perception of infallibility in the minds of the general American populace. This has prompted many U.S. citizens to be insular and uninformed about the rest of the world.* Consequently, there has been less possibility for American students to even begin to see other perspectives. Clearly, American students need to have more than a cursory U.S. approved understanding of life and ways of living, if they are to pursue the level of excellence in learning that will make it possible for them to interact as participants in a global society.

It is important that you develop students' cultural knowledge by integrating it into your classroom practices in ways that convey your cultural competence. In the process, you should be embracing and avoid focusing only on the differences among groups and individuals, but also on their similarities and interconnectedness. You must also think of each student as an individual, as having cultural group characteristics, and as having of characteristics that make each person part of humanity. Displaying your cultural competence requires that you balance each part with the other because if you look only at the individual, the importance of the cultural group and problems such as racism may be overlooked. Or, if you consider a specific cultural group to the exclusion of considering persons as humans across cultural groups you may miss the interconnectedness that each person has as a human being in an increasingly small world.

Understanding the "other" in ways that foster interrelatedness, interdependence, and caring are a major theme of this professional development series. Excellence in student learning follows when we operate from the basic premise that the other person's perspective is to be sought, recognized, and appreciated. James Banks (Banks, 1991) uses the term global competency to describe persons who have attained this level of excellence in cultural knowledge. He sees these persons as having internalized the values and principles of humankind and therefore they are able to act on their values to function effectively both nationally and internationally.

A diverse group of classroom teachers was asked to discuss their views of critical pedagogy and its impact on their classroom philosophy.

Classroom Teachers Talk It Over

"Critical pedagogy is an interesting and enlightening concept. The critical pedagogy cycle can help me fully understand aspects of cultural differentiation. It begins with learning the basics of something early on, then you relearn the material in more depth. Finally, based on new learning you unlearn what you originally learned because it no longer fits."

"Schools and the way classrooms operate have not changed with the times. If teachers were more open to the critical pedagogy mindset, they would see that there are new and alternative ways of approaching classroom practice that are culturally sensitive. Most teachers operate under the "deal with everyone the same way" approach, and that mindset doesn't work any more. There are so many different cultures and beliefs present in today's classrooms that teachers need to open their eyes and see the possibilities for the future."

"Critical pedagogy gives teachers the ability to see beyond what is happening now and look into new happenings. It is looking deeply into situations instead of taking things on face value. Critical pedagogy can help me go beyond what traditional history books say about schools, students, and their cultures and begin to view classrooms through students' eyes and cultural frame of reference. It can also help me create a more respectful place for my students to learn simply by better understanding their perspectives. I believe to really use critical pedagogy I will have to unlearn what I thought I knew and relearn the reality of today's classrooms."

"Critical pedagogy challenges the accepted social order and dares to intervene with a broader more embracing philosophy of classroom practice as a basis for a more enlightened humane society."

As you conclude this module, consider the views of these teachers and be prepared to give your view? How do your thoughts about critical pedagogy compare with the views expressed by these classroom teachers?

A Summary of Learning in Module Three

This module has presented and explained a new perspective to help you examine current classroom management practices. In review, some specific points are:

- This module has focused on explaining critical pedagogy as a way of thinking about current classroom practices and of moving toward a more enlightened perspective. The cycle of learning, relearning, and unlearning forms the essence of the thinking and growth process as you move from what is to what can be. Critical Pedagogy as a way of thinking is to serve as a guide to help you to develop your classroom philosophy.

- You have been introduced to a set of concepts and terminology that form the core of critical pedagogy. Such concepts as conscientization are descriptive constructs, in this case, to express the idea of knowing that you know, and of acting on your knowledge as a matter of conscience. Other terms and concepts help you to see more clearly the relationship between the dominant and non-dominant culture perspectives.

- You have learned how to apply critical pedagogy to examine traditional school practices, why they inhibit cultural understanding, and the implications for you in your role as classroom teacher. For example, when you conclude that such practices as tracking are inhibiting classroom practices, what do you do about it? Not all classroom practices are within your control, but many are. In any event, critical pedagogy teaches you to be an informed intellectual and challenge the assumptions behind what goes on in classrooms rather than compliantly accepting what is.

- Critical pedagogy has helped you to understand the "hidden curriculum" as an informal source of conveying the dominant culture. You are called upon to examine and use this curriculum as a force for good by explicitly teaching the hidden qualities of this curriculum to enable all students to have access to the codes and methods of the dominant culture. This is referred to in this series as teaching the "culture of power" so that non-dominant culture students are not hindered in mainstream society.

- The module discusses ways to overcome the impediments to building cross-cultural understanding as a basis for excellence in student learning. Openness to becoming informed about the rest of the world is a beginning step to understanding other cultures on their terms. The ability to employ multiple perspectives as an avenue to gain a deeper understanding and appreciation of the differences, similarities, and interdependence of people living together leads to cross-cultural understanding and the global knowledge that produces excellence in student learning.

Critical pedagogy, a philosophical orientation and way of thinking, is the driving force behind this module. The approach can be the basis for forming your classroom philosophy. It calls for you to move beyond your comfort zone and traditional way of thinking and being. It asks you to take what you have learned so far, and then to look beyond the margins and between the lines, and adopt a critical eye and new philosophical orientation toward things as they are…

This module concludes Volume One, the context for classroom practice, which has focused on giving you the background and thinking that is necessary to display cultural competence in conducting your classroom. You should now know how culture and classroom practice are interconnected, the historical context and impact of the dominant culture in relationship to other cultures in American schools, and you should be able to employ critical pedagogy to assess classroom practices. Critical pedagogy has served as a process to help you think about the issues surrounding today's schools and discover how certain practices are in conflict with cross-cultural understanding and excellence in student learning. This background sets the stage for you to be a thoughtful culturally-enlightened classroom teacher. At this point in your study, you should have considerable insight into a range of generally accepted classroom practices that you will now want to reconsider and some well-considered thoughts and plans that you will incorporate in your classroom.

The knowledge and insights you have gained in this volume are sure to facilitate a change in your way of thinking about your classroom and the practices you employ, and it could be the only source that you need to improve your classroom practice. However, to obtain more guidance and practical strategies to further develop your cultural knowledge and skill in classroom management, curriculum and teaching, and overall expertise in classroom practice, Volumes II, III, and IV will refer to and build on the cultural context developed in this volume. This volume, the first in the series, is the essential tool to help you formulate a way of thinking about classrooms so that you will benefit fully from the remaining practical volumes in the series.

Opening Scenario (Afterthoughts)

How would you assess the Thanksgiving celebration in the case after studying the material in Module Three? Please give examples to explain some alternative approaches that you will use in your classroom.

The following questions, exercises, and activities will help you assess your level of cultural competence upon completion of Module Three.

Questions/Activities

1. State what critical pedagogy means in terms of your assessment of the dominant American culture. Discuss the language associated with it and how you will use cultural pedagogy in formulating a broader more encompassing perspective that would lead to cross-cultural understanding.

2. What are some typical school practices that inhibit cross-cultural understanding? How will you address such practices in your classroom?

3. What is the history behind the celebration of patriotic holidays such as Columbus Day and Thanksgiving Day in American classrooms? How have these celebrations affected cultural groups other than the dominant mainstream culture? In what ways would you handle these practices in your classroom to respect cultural diversity?

4. Explain the following concepts in relationship to the history of the dominant mainstream culture in America:

Transformative knowledge	sanitizing	sustaining ambivalence
emancipatory knowledge	perspective taking	dialectic
culture of power	voice	double consciousness

5. How does Lisa Delpit view the "culture of power" and how can her approach to directly teaching students the rules and codes of the culture of power be used in classroom practice?

6. What part does empathy play in developing cross-cultural understanding? Explain how you would incorporate perspective taking in your classroom.

7. Summarize the new ideas, principles, and concepts that you learned in this module and explain how you will implement your new insights in your classroom.

Cooperative Group Activity:

Plan a discussion on the terms and concepts associated with critical pedagogy as a way of analyzing the way that schools currently operate. Place emphasis on the ways in which critical pedagogy helps you to formulate a philosophical perspective on conducting your classroom.

Looking in Classrooms

Visit a classroom in your area for the purpose of finding out how the teachers address cultural diversity in relationship to what you have learned in this chapter. Observe and note the following. (Ask questions of the teachers in areas where you need clarification):

1. How culturally diverse are the students in the classroom? What does the classroom setting convey about cultural diversity?

2. Explain your use of critical pedagogy to examine school practices. To what extent are you practicing critical pedagogy? Does the teacher practice critical pedagogy? How do you know?

3. Upon observing the teachers' styles of interacting with students, is there evidence of attention being given to the "culture of power." Please explain.

4. What practices can you detect that would inhibit cross-cultural understanding? What practices would enhance multiple perspectives and promote a caring classroom community?

Following your visitation, write a Brief Descriptive Summary Statement to explain what you observed in this setting, describing any inhibiting practices that you found and what you would do in your own classroom to enhance cross-cultural understanding.

Recommendations for Further Reading

Freire P. *Literacy, Reading the Word and World.* South Hadley, MN: Bergin and Grady, 1987.
This book is a classic in critical pedagogy. It is a must read for those interested in the origins of critical pedagogy.

Giroux, H., A. *Teachers as Intellectuals: Toward a Critical Pedagogy of Learning.* Gransby, Mass: Bergin and Garvey Publishers, Inc., 1988.
This book sets forth a comprehensive theory of critical pedagogy and its manifestations in schools. Giroux calls for teachers to be intellectuals who are not content to accept the status quo in schools.

McLaren, Peter. *Life in Schools: An Introduction in the Foundations of Education,* 5th ed. Los Angeles: Pearson, 2007.
This book builds on earlier theories of critical pedagogy and offers current insights and applications of the theory.

Wink, Joan. *Critical Pedagogy: Notes from the Real World.* Boston: Pearson, 2005.
Joan Wink presents practical applications of critical pedagogy theory. The language of critical pedagogy is illuminated in her book.

Singer, A. "Wanted: Theories and Research That Explain Privilege and Oppression in Education and in U.S. Society." *Race, Gender, and Class*, (2001) (1), 27-38.
Singer discusses the social construction of race and ethnicity, race and class, "Whiteness" and "White privilege," unity of the oppressed, and dealing with racism.

The MASS Professional Development Series in Review

This volume of the four-volume series has set forth ways to improve classroom practice to promote excellence in student learning. Educational excellence, as emphasized has been dependent upon having a broader view of schooling than the traditional western-oriented view. Consequently, the focus has been on broadening American classroom practice to build cross-cultural understanding as a requirement for promoting excellence in student learning.

As the cultural context volume for the series, it addressed the ways in which authorities have been going about school improvement in the wrong way, with the wrong paradigm. In the desire to improve the quality of education by pushing harder and mandating tests to assure dominant-culture learning, school officials have overlooked what is so obvious to those who are on the outside of mainstream American culture looking in. The dominant mainstream American culture, upon which American classrooms operate, has excluded other cultures and ways of viewing the world to the extent that many students have seen themselves as outside of the system. This volume explained why many of these students, especially those whose forbears did not make the choice to be part of American culture, have been resistant or reluctant to fully embrace what goes on in American classrooms.

The series calls for teaching all students the dominant American mainstream "culture of power" so that they would have a solid foundation in the elements of American culture. But even if the schools were to succeed in getting all students to fully embrace these elements, student learning outcomes would still be faulty and inadequate for as the series explains, the substance and philosophical underpinnings upon which American schools are based fail to encompass all available knowledge. Learning outcomes are limited to American culture and function to induct all students into the American way of life, a practice which limits what students learn and how they learn it in the context of American classrooms.

Ways to address this limitation appear in Volumes II-IV, the classroom practice volumes of the series, which outline culturally-compatible practices in classroom management, the education program and the teaching process. Each of these volumes discusses in detail with step-by-step procedures, clear strategies and models to present in the simplest manner possible, ways to apply culturally-inclusive principles and concepts in classrooms. Each volume could be considered a distinct entity in terms of its focus and coverage of a respective strand of classroom practice. However, to obtain a complete picture of the principles and the strategies and methods associated with culturally-compatible classroom practices in classroom management, the education program, and the teaching process all volumes are needed.

Even though the cultural phenomenon is highlighted in the four volumes, it becomes clear to readers over the course of the series that culturally-embracing classroom practice is simply effective classroom practice. The practices surely benefit students from non-dominant cultures but they benefit mainstream American students even more. Moreover, it becomes clear that the application of the recommended classroom practices do not require radical change in what was already established as fundamentally sound classroom practice. The necessary change stressed in each of the four volumes of the series is to have teachers become "transforming intellectuals" who think about and analyze what they do, and then act in accordance with truth, accuracy, and cultural inclusiveness in the interest of all students.

The MASS (Model Alternative School Services) *Professional Development Series for Excellence in Teaching and Learning* sets forth a coordinated approach for examining and improving classroom practice. MASS, through its publications and services is thorough and comprehensive in providing materials and assistance based in the needs of individual clients and schools. This professional development series offers principles and strategies to help teachers learn conceptually how to build cross-cultural understanding and encourage excellence in student learning. Whether it is classroom management, the education program, the teaching, or all three of these classroom practice strands, MASS consultants are prepared to help teachers put the conceptual knowledge derived from this professional development series into action in their daily classroom practice.

References, Vol. 1-4

Adler, Mortimer J. *The Paideia Proposal, An Educational Manifesto.* New York: Macmillan, 1982.

Anderson, James D. *The Education of Blacks in the South, 1860-1935.* Chapel Hill: University of North Carolina Press, 1988.

Anderson, L. M.., N. L Brubaker, J, Allerman-Brooks, and G. Duffy. "A Qualitative Study of Seatwork in First-Grade Classrooms." *Elementary School Journal* (1985) 86, 123-140.

Anderson, Richard C., Elfrieda H. Hiebert, Judith A. Scott, and Ian A. G. Wilkinson. *Becoming A Nation of Readers: The Report of the Commission on Reading.* Washington D.C., 1985.

Apple, M. *Official Language: Democratic Education in a Conservative Age.* New York: Routledge, 1993.

Baloche, Lynda. *The Cooperative Classroom: Empowering Learning.* Upper Saddle River, New Jersey: Prentice Hall, 1998.

Bandura, Albert. *Self Efficacy: The Exercise of Control.* New York: Freeman, 1997.

Bandura, Albert. *Social Foundations of Thought and Action: A Social Cognitive Theory.* Upper Saddle River, New Jersey: Prentice Hall, 1986.

Bandura, Albert. *Social Learning Theory.* Upper Saddle River, N.J.: Prentice Hall, 1977.

Banks, James. *An Introduction to Multicultural Education.* Boston: Allyn and Bacon, 2002.

Banks, James. "Multicultural Literacy and Curriculum Reform," *Educational Horizons,* 69 (3), 135-140.

Banks, James, McGee, and C. Banks, eds. *Multicultural Education: Issues and Perspectives*, Hoboken, NJ: Wiley, 2004.

Bennett, Christine I. *Comprehensive Multicultural Education, 6th ed.* Boston: Pearson Education, 2007.

Berger, Eugenia H. *Parents as Partners in Education: Families and Schools Working Together.* Upper Saddle River, Inc.: Pearson, Merrill, Prentice Hall, 2004.

Bergstrom, A., L. M. Cleary, and Peacock. *Seventh Generation: Native Students Speak About Finding the Good Path.* Charleston, WV: ERIC Clearinghouse on Rural Education and Small Schools, 2003.

Berlin, Ira. *Many Thousands Gone: The First Two Centuries of Slavery in North America.* Cambridge MA: Harvard University Press, 1998.

Bloom, Benjamin S. *Human Characteristics and School Learning.* New York: McGraw-Hill, 1976.

Bloom, Benjamin, ed. *Developing Talent in Young People.* New York: Ballantine Books, 1985.

Brophy, Jere. "Successful Teaching Strategies for the Inner City Child." *Phi Delta Kappa* (1982) 63, 527-530.

Brophy, Jere. "Synthesis of Research on Strategies for Motivating Students to Learn." *Educational Leadership* (1987) 45, 2, 40-48.

Brophy, Jere. and M. McCoslin. "Teachers' Reports of How They Perceive and Cope with Problem Students." *Elementary School Journal* 93, 1 (1992): 3-68.

Brown, Dee. *Bury My Heart at Wounded Knee: An Indian History of the American West.* New York: Holt, 1970.

Bruer, John. *Schools for Thought.* Cambridge, MA: MIT Press, 1993.

Bruner, Jerome S. *The Culture of Education.* Cambridge: Harvard University Press, 1996.

Bruner, Jerome S. *The Process of Education.* Cambridge Mass.: Harvard University Press, 1963.

Charles, C. M. *Building Classroom Discipline.* Boston: Allyn and Bacon, 2002.

Charles, C. M. *Essential Elements of Effective Discipline.* Boston: Allyn and Bacon, 2002.

Chester, M. D. and B. J. Beaudin. "Efficacy Beliefs of Newly Hired Teachers in Urban Schools." *American Research Journal* 33, 1 (1996): 233-257.

Clayton, J. B. *One Classroom, Many Worlds: Teaching and Learning in the Cross-Cultural Classroom.* Portsmouth, NH: Heinemann, 2003.

Coleman, Daniel. *Emotional Intelligence.* New York: Bantam Books, 1995.

Coleman, Michael C. *Presbyterian Missionary Attitudes toward American Indians, 1837-1893.* Jackson: University of Mississippi, 1985

Coloroso, Barbara. *Kids are Worth It.* New York: Harper Collins. 2002.

Cremin, Lawrence. *American Educator: The Colonial Experience 1607-1783.* New York: Harper and Row, 1970.

Cremin, Lawrence. *The American Common School: An Historic Conception.* New York: Teachers College Press, 1951.

Crow, Tracy M. "The Necessity of Diversity." *Journal of Staff Development* 29, no.1 (Winter, 2008): 54-58.

Cruickshank, Donald, Deborah Jenkins, and Kim Metcalf. *The Act of Teaching.* 4th ed. Boston: McGraw-Hill, 2007.

Cummins, James. "Negotiating Identities: Education for Empowerment in a Diverse Society." *California Association for Bilingual Education,* Ontario, CA, 1996.

D'Angelo, Raymond. *Taking Sides—Clashing Views in Race and Ethnicity, 6th ed.* Dubuque, Iowa: McGraw-Hill, 2008.

Darling-Hammond Land J. Bransford. *Preparing Teachers for a Changing World: What Teachers Should Learn and Be Able to Do.* San Francisco: Jossey Bass, 2005.

Delpit, Lisa. *Other Peoples Children: Cultural Conflict in the Classroom.* New York: The New Press, 1995.

Dewey, John. *Experience and Education.* New york: MacMillan/Collier, 1938.

Doyle, W. "Classroom Organization and Management." In M. Wittrock, ed. *Handbook of Research on Teaching, 3rd ed.* 392-431. New York: Macmillan, 1986.

Doyle, W. *Classroom Management Techniques in O. C. Moles (Ed.), Student Discipline Strategies: Research and Practice.* Albany State University of New York Press, 1990.

Du Bois, W.E.B. *The Souls of Black Folk.* New York: Penguin Books, USA, Inc., 1961.

Duffy, T. and D. Cunningham. "Constructivism: Implications for the Design and Delivery of Instruction." D. Jonassen, ed. *Handbook of Research for Educational Communications and Technology.* New York: Macmillan, 1996.

Duit, R. "Students Conceptual Frameworks: Consequences for Learning in Science." In S. M. Glynn, R. H. Yeany, &B. K. Britton (Eds.), *The Psychology of Learning Science.* Hillsdale, NJ: Erlbaum, 1991.

Eby, Judy. *Reflective Planning, Teaching, and Evaluation for the Elementary School.* New York: Prentice Hall, 2001.

Edmonds, Ronald R. A Discussion of the Literature and Issues Related to Effective Schooling. Cambridge, MA: Center for Urban Studies, Harvard Graduate School of Education, 1979a.

Edmonds, Ronald R. *Making Public Schools Effective.* Social Policy 12 (2), 1981.

Eisenhower, J. S. D. *So Far from God: The U.S. War with Mexico 1846-1848.* New York: Anchor Books, 1989.

Eisner, Eliot. W. *The Educational Imagination: On the Design and Evaluation of School Programs (3rd ed.).* New York: Macmillan, 1994.

Emmer, Edmond T. and Carolyn Evertson. Teacher's Manual for the Junior High Classroom Management Improvement Study. Austin: R&D Center for Teacher Education, University of Texas, 1981.

Emmer, Edmond T. and Carolyn Evertson. *Classroom Management for Middle and High School Teachers, 8th ed..* New Jersey: Pearson, 2009.

Fisher, C., D. Berliner, N. Filby, R. Marliave, L. Cahen, and M. Dishaw. "Teaching Behaviors, Academic Learning Time, and Student Achievement: An Overview." In C. Denham and Lieberman (Eds.), *Time to Learn.* Washington D.C.: Dept of Education, 1980.

Epstein, Joyce L. & M. G. Sanders. "Family, School, and Community Partnerships." In M. Bornstein (Ed.), *Handbook of Parenting (2nd ed.).* Mahwah, NJ: Lawrence Erlbaum, 2002.

Francis, Paul P. *The Great Father: The United States Government and the American Indians.* Lincoln: University Press, 1984.

Freire, Paolo. *Pedagogy of the Oppressed.* New York: Continuum, 1970.

Freire, Paolo. *Education for Critical Consciousness.* New York: Continuum, 1973.

Freire Paolo. *Literacy, Reading the Word and World.* South Hadley, MN: Bergin and Grady, 1987.

Garcia, E. *Student Cultural Diversity: Understanding and Meeting the Challenge, 2nd ed.* Boston: Houghton Mifflin, 1999.

Gardner, Howard. *Frames of Mind: The Theory of Multiple Intelligences.* New York: Basic Books, 1993.

Gay, Geneva, ed., *Becoming Multicultural Educators.* Hoboken, New Jersey: John Wiley and Sons, 2003.

Genovese, Eugene D. *Roll Jordan Roll: The World the Slaves Made.* New York: Vintage Books, 1972.

Geertz, C. *The Interpretation of Cultures.* New York: Basic Books, 1973.

Giroux, Henry. A. *Teachers as Intellectuals: Toward a Critical Pedagogy of Learning.* Granby, Mass.: Bergin and Garvey Publishers, Inc., 1988.

Giroux, Henry. A. *Resisting Difference: Cultural Studies and the Discourse of Critical Pedagogy.* Philadelphia: Routledge, 1992.

Glasser, William. *The Quality School.* New York: Harper and Row Publishers, 1990.

Gollnick, Donna M. and Phillip C. Chinn. *Multicultural Education in a Pluralistic Society.* Pearson: New Jersey, 2006.

Gonzalez, Gilbert. *Chicano Education in the Era of Segregation.* Philadelphia: Balch Institute Press, 1990.

Good, Thomas and T. Beckerman. "Time on Task: A Naturalistic Study in Sixth Grade Classrooms," *The Elementary School Journal.* (1978) 78, 193-201.

Good, Thomas L. and Jere E. Brophy. *Looking in Classrooms, 8th ed.* New York: Addison Wesley Longman, Inc., 2000.

Goodlad, John. *A Place Called School, 20th Anniversary ed.* New York: McGraw-Hill, 2004.

Grant, Carl, ed. *Research and Multicultural Education: From the Margins to the Mainstream.* London: The Palmer Press, 1992.

Grant, Carl, and Maureen Gillette. *Learning to Teach Everyone's Children.* California: Thomson Wadsworth, 2006.

Guadalupe, San Miguel, Jr. *Let All of Them Take Heed: Mexican Americans and the Campaign for Educational Equality in Texas, 1910-1981.* Austin: University of Texas Press, 1987.

Gunstone, R. F., and R. T. White. "Understanding of Gravity," *Science Education.* 1981, 65, 291-299.

Hall, Edward T. *The Silent Language.* Greenwich, Ct.: Fawcett, 1959.

Harris, Ian, M. "Peace Education in a Violent Culture." *Harvard Educational Review* 77, no.3 (Fall, 2007): 350-354.

Hartzopovlos, Maria. "Deepening Democracy: How One School's Fairness Committee Offers an Alternative to Discipline," *Rethinking Schools*, 21, no.1 (Fall, 2006): 42-43.

Helms, J. "Why Is There No Study of Cultural Equivalence in Standardized Cognitive Ability Testing?" *American Psychologist.* 47, 9, (1992): 1083-1101.

Hirsch, E..D. Jr. *Cultural Literacy.* New York: Vintage Books, 1987.

Hofstede, Geert. *Culture's Consequence: International Differences in Work-Related Values.* Beverly Hills, CA: Sage, 1984.

Hunter, Madeline. *Mastery Teaching.* Thousand Oaks, CA: Corwin Press, 1982.

Jackson Lears, Thomas J. *No Place of Grace: Anti Modernism and the Transformation of American Culture 1880-1920.* University of Missouri Press, Columbia Missouri, 1981.

Jacobs, H.H. *Mapping the Big Picture: Integrating Curriculum and Assessment K-12.* Alexandria Virginia: Association for Supervision and Curriculum Development, 1997.

Hom, A, & V. Battistich. "Students' Sense of School Community as a Factor in Reducing Drug Use and Delinquency." Paper Presented at the Annual Meeting of the American Educational Research Association, San Francisco, 1995.

Joshi, Arti, Jody Eberly, & Jean Konzal. "Dialogue Across Cultures: Teachers' Perceptions About Communication with Diverse Families." *Multicultural Education.* 13, no. 2 (December, 2005):11-15.

Johnson, David W. and Roger T. Johnson. *Circles of Learning: Cooperation in the Classroom, 5th ed.* Arlington, Virginia: Association for Supervision and Curriculum Development, 1984.

Kaestle, Carl F. *Pillars of the Republic: Common Schools and American Society 1780-1860.* New York: Hill and Wang, 1983.

Kim, D, D. Solomon, & W. Roberts. "Classroom Practices That Enhance Students Sense of Community." Paper Presented at the Annual Meeting of the American Educational Research Association, San Francisco, 1995.

Kimball, S. T. *Culture and the Educative Process.* New York: Teachers College Press, 1974.

Klopf, Donald W. *Intercultural Encounters: The Fundamentals of Intercultural Communication.* Englewood, Co.: Morton Publishing Co., 1991.

Kohlberg, Lawrence. "Essays on Moral Development." *The Psychology of Moral Development.* 2. New York: Harper and Row, 1984.

Kohlberg, Lawrence. *The Psychology of Moral Development: The Nature and Validity of Moral Stages.* San Francisco: Harper and Rowe, 1984.

Kohn, Alfie. *Punished by Rewards.* New York: Houghton Mifflin Co., 1993.

Kounin, Jacob. *Group Management in Classrooms.* New York: Holt, Rinehart, Winston, Inc., 1970.

Kozol, Jonathan. *The Night is Dark and I am Far from Home.* New York: Simon and Schuster, 1975.

Kuhn, D., E. Amsel, & M. O'Loughlin. *The Development of Scientific Thinking Skills.* San Diego, Academic Press, 1988.

Ladson-Billings, Gloria. *The Dream Keepers: Successful Teachers of African American Children.* San Francisco: Jossey Bass, 1994.

Ladson-Billings, Gloria. "Preparing Teachers for Diverse Populations: A Critical Race Theory Perspective." In A, Iran-Nejd & P.D. Pearson (Eds.), *Review of Research in Education,* 24. Washington, D.C. American Educational Research Association, 1999.

Lansford, Jennifer. "Educating American Students for Life in a Global Society." *Center for Child and Family Policy* 2, no.4 (2002): 1-3.

Lee, James L., Charles J. Pulvino, and Philip A. Perrone. *Restoring Harmony, A Guide to Managing Schools.* Upper Saddle River, New Jersey: Prentice Hall, 1998.

Lee, Robert G. Orientals: *Asian Americans in Popular Culture.* Philadelphia: Temple University Press, 1999.

Lee, Seungyoun, and Mary Ellen Dallman. "Engaging in a Reflective Examination about Diversity: Interviews with Three Pre-service Teachers." *Multicultural Education.* 15, no. 4 (July 1, 2008): 36-44.

Lemann, Nicholas. *The Promised Land: The Great Black Migration and How It Changed America.* New York: Vintage Books, 1991.

Levine, Lawrence W. *Black Culture and Black Consciousness: African American Folk Thought from Slavery to Freedom.* New York: Oxford University Press, 1977.

Likona, Thomas. *Educating for Character.* New York: Bantam Books, 1991.

Likona, Thomas. *Raising Good Children: From Birth Through the Teen Age Years.* New York: Bantam Books, 1983.

Manning, M. L. and L. G. Baruth. *Multicultural Education of Children and Adolescents.* Boston: Allyn and Bacon, 2004.

Marx, Sherry, and Julie Pennington. "Pedagogies of Critical Race Theory: Experimentations with White Preservice Teachers." *Qualitative Studies in Education.* 16, no. 1 (2003): 91-110.

Marzano, Robert J., Debra J. Pickering, and J. McTighe. *Assessing Student Outcomes: Performance Assessment Using the Dimensions of Learning Model.* McREL Institute. Aurora, CO, 1993.

Marzano, Robert J. *What Works in Schools: Translating Research into Action.* Alexandria, VA: Association for Supervision and Curriculum Development, 2002-2003.

McEwan, Barbara. *The Art of Classroom Management: Effective Practices for Building Learning Communities.* Upper Saddle River, NJ: Prentice Hall, 2000.

McGreal, Thomas. *Successful Teacher Evaluation.* Alexandria, VA: Association for Supervision and Curriculum Development. 1983.

McLaren, Peter. *Life in Schools: An Introduction in the Foundations of Education, 5th ed.* Los Angeles: Pearson, 2007.

McLaughlin, W. G. *Cherokee Renascence in the New Republic.* Princeton: University of Princeton Press, 1986.

Ming, Kavin and Charles Dukes. "Fostering Cultural Competence Through School-Based Routines." *Multicultural Education* 14, no.1 (Fall, 2006): 42-49.

Mitchell, Diana. *Children's Literature, An Invitation to the World.* Boston, MA: Allyn and Bacon, 2003.

Monroe, Carla. "Understanding the Discipline Gap through a Cultural Lens: Implications for the Education of African American Students." *Intercultural Education* 16, no. 4 (October, 2005): 317-330.

Moore, John H. *The Emergence of the Cotton Kingdom in the Old Southwest: Mississippi 1770-1860.* Baton Rouge: Louisiana State University Press, 1988.

Nieto, Sonia. *Affirming Diversity: The Sociopolitical Context of Multicultural Education.* New York: Addison Wesley Longman, 2000.

Noddings, Nell. *The Challenge to Care in Schools: An Alternative Approach to Education.* New York: Teachers College Press, 1992.

Noddings, Nell. "Competence and Caring As Central to Teacher Education." Paper presented at the Annual meeting of the American Research Association. Montreal, 1999.

Noddings, Nell, ed. *Educating Citizens for Global Awareness.* New York: Teachers College Press, 2005.

Noddings, Nell. "Teaching the Themes of Care." *Phi Delta Kappan,* 76, (1995): 675-679.

Nuhlicek, Allan. "Relationship of School Boundary Conditions, Gemeinschaft Conditions, and Student Achievement Scores in Reading and Mathematics in Selected Milwaukee Public Schools." Ph.D. diss., Marquette University. Milwaukee, Wisconsin, 1981.

Oakes, Jeannie. *Keeping Track: How Schools Structure Inequality.* New Haven, CT: Yale University Press, 1999.

Oakes, Jeannie and Martin Lipton. *Teaching to Change the World (2nd ed.).* Boston: McGraw-Hill, 2003.

Obeakor, Festus E.. *It Even Happens in Good Schools: Responding to Cultural Diversity In Today's Classrooms.* CA: Corwin Press, 2001.

Ogbu, John. "Cultural Discontinuities and Schooling," *Anthropology and Education Quarterly*, 13, no.4, (1982): 290-307.

Ogbu, John. *Minority Status and Schooling: A Comparative Study of Immigrant and Involuntary Minorities.* New York: Garland, 1991.

Ogbu, John. "Understanding Cultural Diversity and Learning." *Educational Researcher* 21, no.8 (1992): 5-14.

Pai, Y., S. Adler, and L. K. Shadiow. *Cultural Foundations of Education.* Upper Saddle River: Pearson Education, Inc., 2006.

Pai, Y. S., and D. Pemberton. *Findings on Korean American Early Adolescents and Adolescents.* University of Missouri: Kansas City MO, 1987.

Palincsar, A. and A. Brown. "Reciprocal Teaching of Comprehension Monitoring Activities." *Cognition and Instruction* 2 (1984): 117-175.

Perkins, David and T. Blythe. "Putting Understanding Up Front." *Educational Leadership* 51, no. 4 (1992): 4-7.

Perrone, V. ed. *Expanding Student Assessment.* Alexandria, VA: Association for Supervision and Curriculum Development, 1991.

Pewewardy, C. "Learning Styles of American Indian/Alaska Native Students: A Review of Literature and Implications for Practice." *Journal of American Indian Education*, 41 (3), 22-56.

Piaget, Jean. *The Child's Conception of the World.* New York: Harcourt Brace, 1929.

Piaget, Jean. *Origins of Intelligence in Children.* New York: International Universities Press, 1952.

Pickett, Linda. "Diversity Education: Respect, Equality, and Social Justice." *Childhood Education* 84, no. 3 (Spring, 2008): 158.

Power, F.Clark, Ann Higgins, and Lawrence Kohlberg. *Lawrence Kohlberg's Approach to Moral Education.* New York: Columbia University Press, 1989.

Ravitch, Diane. *The Troubled Crusade: American Education, 1945-1980.* New York: Basic Books, 1983.

Ray, Katie. W. "Reading Aloud: Filling the Room with the Sound of Wondrous Words," *Wondrous Words: Writers and Writing in the Elementary Classroom.* NCTE, 1999.

Redfield, Robert. "The Contribution of Anthropology to the Education of Teachers." In F. A. J. Ianni & E. Storey (Eds.) *Cultural Relevance and Educational Issues,* (153-159). Boston: Little, Brown, 1973.

Resnick, Lauren. *Education and Learning to Think.* Washington D.C.: National Academy Press, 1987.

Resnick, Lauren. and I. Klopfer. "Toward the Thinking Curriculum: An Overview." In Resnick and Kloepfer, eds. *Toward the Thinking Curriculum: Current Cognitive Research.* (1989): 1-18.

Reyhner, J., and J. Eder. *American Indian Education: A History.* Norman OK: University of Oklahoma Press, 2004.

Rosenshine, Barak. "How Time Is Spent in Elementary Schools." In C. Denham and A. Lieberman, eds. *Time to Learn.* Washington, D.C.: Department of Education, 1980.

Rosenshine, Barak. "Teaching Functions in Instructional Programs." *The Elementary School Journal,* 83, (1983): 335-351.

Rowe, Mary B. "Wait Time, Slowing Down May be A Way of Speeding Up." *American Educator* 11, (Spring, 1987): 38-43, 47.

Shor, Ira. *Empowering Education: Critical Teaching for Social Change.* Chicago: University of Chicago Press, 1992.

Shor, Ira., and Paolo Freire. *A Pedagogy for Liberation: Dialogues on Transforming Education.* South Hadley, MA: Bergin & Garvey, 1987.

Short, Kathy G., Kathryn Pierce, and Mitchell Pierce, eds. *Talking About Books: Creating Literate Communities,* Portsmouth, New Hampshire: Heinemann Educational Books, 1990.

Sizer, Theodore. *Horace's Compromise: The Dilemma of the American High School.* Boston: Houghton-Mifflin, 1984.

Skinner, B. F. *Science and Human Behavior.* New York: Macmillan, 1953.

Sleeter, Christine, ed. *Empowerment through Multicultural Education.* New York: State University of New York Press, 1991.

Smith, Rogers. *Civic Ideals: Conflicting Visions of Citizenship in U. S. History.* New Haven: Yale University Press, 1997.

Sokolower, Jody. "Bringing Globalization Home, A High School Teacher Helps Immigrant Students Draw on Their Own Expertise." *Rethinking Schools,* 21, no.1 (Fall, 2006): 46-48.

Spindler, G. and I Spindler. *The American Cultural Dialogue and Its Transmission.* New York: Palmer Press, 1990.

Spindler, G. D., "Education in a Transforming America." In G. D. Spindler (Ed.), *Education and Culture* (132-147). New York: Holt, Reinhart, and Winston, 1963.

Spring, Joel. *The American School 1642-2004.* New York: McGraw-Hill, 2005.

Spring, Joel. *Conflict of Interests: The Politics of American Education.* New York: McGraw-Hill, 2005.

Spring, Joel. *Deculturalization and the Struggle for Equality: Dominated Cultures in the United States, 5th ed.* New York: McGraw Hill, 2006.

Stein, S. J. The Culture of Education Policy. New York: Teachers College Policy, 2005.

Stokes, Sandra. "A Partnership for Creating a Multicultural Teaching Force: A Model for the Present." *Multicultural Education* 7, no.1 (Fall, 1999): 8-12.

Strong, R. W., Silver. H.F., and Perini, M.J. *Teaching What Matters Most: Standards and Strategies for Raising Student Achievement.* Alexandria, VA: Association for Supervision and Curriculum Development, 2001.

Takaki, Ronald. *A Different Mirror: A History of Multicultural America.* Boston: Little Brown and Company, 1993.

Taylor, George R., ed. *Practical Applications of Classroom Management Theories into Strategies.* Dallas: University Press of America, 2004.

Thompson, Gail L. *The Power of One: How You Can Help or Harm African American Students.* CA: Corwin Press, 2010.

Tyler, Ralph. *Basic Principles of Curriculum and Instruction.* Chicago: University of Chicago Press, 1949.

Vang, Christopher T. "Minority Parents Should Know More about School Culture and Its Impact on Their Children's Education." *Multicultural Education.* 14, no. 3 (April 1, 2007): 32-40.

Vygotsky, Lev S. *Mind in Society: The Development of Higher Psychological Processes.* Cambridge, MA: Harvard University Press, 1978.

Wang, M.C., G.D. Haertel & H.J. Wahlberg "What Helps Students Learn?" *Educational Leadership*, (1993/1994) 51(4), 74-79.

Whitehead, Alfred N. *The Aims of Education and Other Essays.* New York: Free Press, 1929.

Wiggins, Grant. "Practicing What We Preach in Designing Authentic Assessment." *Educational Leadership*, 54, 4 (1996-1997): 18-25.

Wiggins, Grant & Jay McTighe. *Understanding by Design.* Arlington, VA: Association for Supervision and Curriculum Development, 1998.

Wink, Joan. *Critical Pedagogy: Notes from the Real World.* Boston: Pearson, 2005.

Wong, Harry K. and Rosemary T. Wong. *The First Days of School.* California: Harry T. Wong Publications, 1998.

Zinn, Howard. *A Peoples History of the United States 1492-Present.* New York: Harper Collins, 1999.

Advanced Praise for MASS Professional Development Series

Many of the concepts and principles expressed throughout this Professional Development series were initiated at Bruce-Guadalupe Community School where Dr. Newsome provided consultant services over a five year period to our culturally diverse Latino-American school. The practices were well received by the faculty, community, and students as we opened a new culturally-enriched schooling opportunity for students in the Milwaukee, Wisconsin community. We continue to be grateful to Dr. Newsome for her dedicated work. Readers should find the program which she has outlined in this series to be thoughtful, insightful and practical.

—Walter Sava, Ph.D. Executive Director, Bruce-Guadalupe Community School. Milwaukee, WA

The culturally-centered approach to classroom practice which Dr. Newsome has undertaken in this series is a progressive step forward in pre service and graduate study for our schools of education. It is time to move past the dominant-culture mindset. I agree that we all too often take on the status quo rather than challenging our assumptions and broadening our perspectives about cultures beyond our own. This series is definitely needed in education and beyond.

—Elaine Roberts, Ph.D., Professor, University of West Georgia. Carrollton, GA

Dr. Newsome's unique perspective and approach to classroom practice has been a source of enrichment for me. As a faculty member who worked closely with Dr. Newsome in developing and implementing a key component of this professional development series, I have broadened and systematically incorporated the culturally-transformative approach to teaching in my work with students and into my own teaching repertoire. Readers are sure to change their practices as a result of reading and engaging with the ideas in this series.

—Cathleen Doheny, Ph.D., Professor, Edison State College, Edison, FL

Dr. Newsome's ideas are enlightening to educators everywhere. What I like most about the book series is that it not only covers standard classroom practice, she takes it a step further to discuss how to prepare teachers to operate in a culturally diverse world. She breaks the information down bit by bit in a way that it is extremely understandable to her readers. Her book series is one of my most valuable purchases. I recommend reading it and keeping it as a refresher.

—Mallori Saylor, Student, University of West Georgia, Carrollton, GA

www.ingramcontent.com/pod-product-compliance
Lightning Source LLC
Chambersburg PA
CBHW080550170426
43195CB00016B/2737